Grief *to* GREATNESS

THE ART OF TURNING HEARTBREAK INTO TRIUMPH

TANYA UNKOVICH
Resilience Architect & Transformation Specialist

Published by
BEVERLY HILLS PUBLISHING™
468 N. Camden Drive
Beverly Hills, CA 90210

Beverly Hills Publishing™
www.beverlyhillspublishing.com

ISBN: 979-8-9916455-9-1

Dedication

TO MY PARENTS, PAULINE AND SMILJAN UNKOVICH, WHO BOTH PASSED AWAY DURING THE CREATION OF THIS BOOK.

YOU WERE MY FIRST TEACHERS ON HOW TO BE RESILIENT.

I HONOUR YOU.

I RESPECT YOU.

I THANK YOU.

UNTIL WE MEET AGAIN.

Contents

Part 3: Physical Mastery

Part 4: Loving Again Later in Life

Part 5: My Search for Purpose

Preface

Today is March 1, 2021, and finally, I feel ready to focus on nothing else but writing this book. I commenced in 2010 and have written thousands and thousands of words in the past eleven years. Whilst I was not sure of what this next book would look like, what I did know to do was write.

At one point, I felt the book was complete. It had a completely different title, but then life threw me another massive curveball. Even though I was initially frustrated and angry, I eventually let go, trusting that this book would be complete in time. Eventually, I realized there was much more to experience before I could write it.

April 12, 2021, was my late husband Phil's sixteenth anniversary. In late 2004, on his forty-eighth birthday, just as he was about to cut his cake, he received a phone call informing him that he had cancer. The following morning, we learned that this mysterious lump under his arm was, in fact, secondary to an aggressive cancer already making its way through his body.

The story of Phil's diagnosis, passing, and the twelve months that followed is documented in my first book, *Unplanned Journey, a Triumph in Life and Death.* Phil had a deep desire to write a book about his journey with cancer, and in fact, it was his hope to write about his recovery as well. This was not meant to be - and within weeks of his passing, I knew I needed to write the book for him... and for me.

The entire process of writing this second book progressed naturally, and it was then that I decided to follow my heart and give myself permission to write more of my story.

We all have a purpose in life, and sometimes, it takes a life-altering event to finally find what that is. This was how it unfolded for me. You might be living your journey right now, or perhaps you're still searching for something more meaningful.

There is meaning, purpose, and greatness within all of us. As a child, I had fantasies and dreams of what the future might look like. However, I never for a million years would have believed that my search for meaning and purpose in the world was going to be because of intense loss and grief.

I have had much to deal with and overcome in my life, from deep personal obstacles as a teenager to consequences of bad decisions in my twenties to the deep grief of infertility in my thirties, and then the ultimate blow, widowed at forty. Despite it all, I wasn't prepared to give up on my life or myself.

The morning after Phil's death, I stood in my kitchen looking out at our wonderful vegetable garden, and I said to God, *I don't know what you want, but I believe you have a plan and purpose for me. Soon, I know I will understand the meaning of all that has happened.*

I knew I was here on this earth for a reason. I just needed to take one day at a time and do whatever was before me to fulfill my purpose. One thing I knew for sure was that no matter what, I was determined to see it through.

So, I wrote this book about my journey from grief to greatness. In it, I share many stories of my life with you all, not only since Phil's death but even before that. I dug deep to overcome the deep personal pain I carried for many years in my life. Now I share with you how I healed, and yet how, during the different decades of my life, I had to revisit these same issues.

I share with you how my life completely changed when, at forty, I had to revisit the whole lot, even the things I thought I had dealt with and put to rest. Grief brought the whole lot back. I also share how I triumphed and decided to dig deep within myself.

There is greatness within all of us; however, not only do so many of us not even know what greatness looks or feels like, but we do not allow ourselves to achieve our dreams. We allow life to take over. We drown in heartache, and we give up on ourselves. We believe that it can happen for others but not for ourselves. The saddest part is that we do not believe we are worthy of greatness.

Everything in my life came about because of a decision. Some were good, and some were poor. At least I didn't sit on the fence but kept making more decisions, sometimes to correct the previous bad ones!

In the end, I said yes to me. I said yes to greatness, and whilst many times I had no idea what greatness looked like, I still said yes to moving forward. My hope for you is that once you have read this book, you, too, will say yes to you.

Foreword

It wasn't a career ambition for me to be a politician; however, in 2022, due to the state of our country and the world, for that matter, I made the decision to stand in the next general election in New Zealand.

How easy it would be to remain on the sidelines and throw stones at the elected leaders as we watch our society crumble. Instead, I decided to stop moaning, be brave, and step inside the arena and make the change I so longed for.

October 14, 2023, was the national election in New Zealand, and our small but powerful political party secured enough votes to stand for dramatic change, something the people desperately longed for. In December 2023, I was sworn in as a Member of Parliament in the 54th Parliament of New Zealand, and as I write, I have had the privilege of serving for just over a year in service to our people.

It has been an extraordinary year, one of many lessons. In fact, during the past four years, life has taught me more lessons than I wanted, but clearly, it has been the ones I needed in order to do the work I am now doing.

I could very easily write another book about them all, and maybe one day I will; however, for now, the words to follow will be a summary and the foreword for the book you are about to read.

One thing I know to be true is that no one was spared from suffering in some shape or form throughout this extraordinary time, we all went through it.

Locked down and separated from one another, fear fed to us on a daily basis, and some of us were faced with decisions that we would have never imagined in our lifetime we would be asked to make.

The loss of my parents during this time was my greatest pain. Meeting as teenagers and spending nearly their entire lives together, they were forced to spend much of the past two years of their lives apart. Separated, locked away from their children, their friends, and worst of all, from each other.

One day in August of 2021, my father became suddenly very ill, was hospitalized, and without really knowing what was wrong with him, we were told he would die. My three brothers, all overseas, were forbidden to return home to hold him one more time. Thankfully, as he was taking his final breaths, my father was in my arms, as I repeatedly shouted to him, "I love you, Tata."

On the day of his funeral, our country was once again locked down. Every single citizen, not to be released for many months. He lay in the funeral home for many days until one day we decided he needed to be laid to rest. It didn't look like our lockdown was going to be ending any day soon.

I sang as I stood outside the funeral home and watched my father's hearse being led away, his casket visible. *"Oh Lord my God, when I in awesome wonder,"* I sang. It was only with God's strength that I could cope with the fact that this was all I could do, watch from the side of the road as my father took the three-hour journey up North where he was laid to rest.

The only two people allowed to be present during his burial were the young man who dug his grave, and the funeral director.

I did not get to see my mother for many weeks after my father's death. Not quite fully understanding what had happened, she was left alone in the rest home to grieve the love of her life. My heart ached for my mama, all day, every day, until finally I was "allowed" to see her, and hold her again.

Eight months after the death of my father, I had to face the event I had dreaded all my life, the moment my mother took her final breaths. Thankfully, again, I was with her. Not having children of my own, my parents were everything to me. The solace I had was the fact that she was no longer in pain, and that hopefully, my parents were together again.

I was once told that "no matter what you are facing, there is good in everything." Here I was again in life, facing excruciating pain, and the decision to choose joy over suffering. I knew that good would come of these past years, and it was up to me to create meaning and find purpose. God had a plan, and it was up to me to accept it.

One shining moment was this book finally being completed and published. Also, life led me to meet with an outstanding thought leader, Andrea Albright, the CEO of Beverly Hills Publishing, and together we released my fourth book: *"F*ck the Food: the ladies' guide to letting go."*

Deep within I knew that my contribution to mankind was not yet done. After experiencing the craziness of the pandemic years, the control, the fear, and seeing the aftermath of pain and suffering left in its wake, I made another decision. Politics.

If I wanted to make a true difference in the world, then it had to be done on a greater scale. I removed my head from the political sandbox where it had comfortably rested for way too long, and the decision was made to stand in the next general election in New Zealand.

How I would do this was still a mystery to me, so I just kept taking positive steps forward, focused on the outcome I wanted, and trusted that everything would unfold perfectly, as it did. The short story is, in late 2023, I was sworn in as a Member of Parliament in Government in New Zealand, and this is what now takes up the bulk of my life.

The insecure little girl of immigrant parents, brought up on a farm, was now a woman on a mission. One that felt like an extraordinary, divine journey.

There is most definitely a book within to expand on this journey, however, until then, I hope you enjoy this book, and that it encourages you to rise up in search of your own greatness.

Introduction

There could be a few reasons you have decided to read this book.

It may be that you are currently feeling the loss of a loved one, perhaps your spouse. It is still early days as you fumble around in the darkness of each long day and the numbness of grief that envelops you at night.

Right now, what you need is to read the story of someone else who has taken the same journey and connect with another human being who truly understands your pain. You want to learn how to cope. However, what you most want to know is that one day, your pain will end.

It may be curiosity that has led you to pick up this book. Perhaps you have been diagnosed with a life-altering illness. Maybe the disease is terminal, and you are now on your own unplanned journey. You want to know what your spouse might feel or what it might be like for them when you are gone. Your desire to protect them has already begun. Also, on some level, you have (just between you and me) picked up this book to search for hope, comfort, and peace.

Alternatively, you have picked up this book because you have recovered but are stuck. You are ready to move forward. However, you have no idea what that means or even what it looks like. You have suffered a significant loss in your life. You have spent years in the wilderness and have decided that now is the time to live again. You want to recover your physical health, restore your emotional resilience, reboot your professional life, and maybe, just maybe, be open to loving again. You have made the decision that now is the time not only to explore but also to allow your greatness to flourish.

You may feel that the word *greatness* is bold, brave, and perhaps even arrogant. That is okay. Once upon a time, I felt the same way. However, after many years of holding myself back, stifling my own needs and desires, and keeping myself small, one day, something deep inside me said *no more*!

That day, for me, was the last day of my husband Phil's life, watching him fight for every breath. The most horrific day of my life was also the day I was reborn. I declared I would no longer waste another day of my precious life.

After his diagnosis, Phil began to open up to his greatness. He allowed his authentic self to emerge and shine as he navigated through the fear, the joy, the pain, and ultimately, the peace of his final days.

If you are going through a similar experience, then the purpose of this book is to help you through it. To provide you with the tools to cope with the realities and monotony of your journey and learn how to be present during it. I am here to assist you in facing it, not running from it.

You will learn from my journey after Phil's death that living again is possible, living joyfully with meaning and purpose. If and when you are ready, you will also discover that safely allowing yourself to love again is possible.

I hope that what I share with you in this book will provide a way to make your journey a little less traumatic. I know that by reading this book, I hope to help you not make some of my mistakes and, as a result, save you a lot of time, heartache, and even money.

If you are reading this book because you are curious about how to live a life of greatness, then great! Here is my simple message to you. Begin living it now. You already have everything available to you right now to be happy and live a life of fulfillment. My greatest hope is that you will understand this fact after reading this book.

How many of us wait for *someday* to start living? Do not wait for an extreme event or tragic loss before you wake up. Your life is already beautiful, and it is time to see it.

My life has been a magical mix of experiences, each decade providing a major life lesson, but I had to revisit each lesson during these past sixteen years. I will take you back and forth through the years, sharing stories about the various events that helped build my muscle of resilience.

From the eating and food issues, which began in my teen years, and the self-doubt that led me to make some of my not-so-good decisions in my twenties, I write openly. Whether you are depending on food or alcohol or another substance to cope, I lay bare the struggles in my own life.

My thirties brought confidence, love, and the darkness of facing real grief. From the diagnosis of my Dad and then Mom, plus having to face the excruciating pain that infertility brings, I will share it with you.

It was the journey through my forties that shook my world and identity and is what taught me the true meaning of resilience. I share with you parts of my journey in finding purpose and myself after Phil's death, healing all those parts within me that I thought were broken, and eventually finding love again.

For ease of flow, I have divided this book into seven parts, one for each of my pillars of resilience. Within each part, I share my stories, events, and adversity. However, I also share with you how I overcame each and continue to reach for mastery in these areas of my life.

As I ask many powerful questions throughout this book, I invite you to purchase your notebook to document what is in your heart as you read.

With years of education in commerce, counseling, personal training, and life coaching, I am qualified to speak and teach. It is, however, my life experiences and recovery from addiction, abuse, grief, and emotional suffering that I feel more qualified to share with you. With absolute certainty, the solutions I present have worked for me, and I know they will work for you, too, if you are ready to let go and step out on a new adventure.

No matter what is happening for you right now, what level of suffering you are feeling, know this: everything you need to overcome your pain and pass through it is right in front of you. I will show you how to notice, embrace, and run with it.

Part I

• Emotional Greatness – Taking the Journey Within •

Chapter: 1

Everything Begins with a Decision

I won't deny that I am glad I didn't realize the journey ahead of me after Phil passed away. During that first year, there were many times I did not want to live. I couldn't imagine living the remainder of my life this way. There were also times when I had unstoppable belief in myself and that all my years of personal development and my resilient nature would get me through.

I also had absolute faith that there was a bigger plan for me. Whilst I had no idea what that looked like, nor how it would materialize, having this deep knowing inside was enough. It kept me going as long as I held on to the belief that there was something beyond the horizon I could not even imagine.

What I did know was that the only way to work through my grief was to walk through it. There was no way around it, only through it. Making that decision was vital. Knowing I had what it took inside - enabled me to get up each day and take those first steps even when I didn't want to.

I knew I was resilient, bold, and determined not to settle for a mediocre life. I had always been curious as to why I felt the way I did and knew that even though I was thrown into grief when I least expected it, I held on to the fact that I could conquer with faith. My trust in God was that great.

If I were to give you my secret about how I have come through everything that life has presented me, it is that I have learned how to manage my personal state of being. It is *everything*.

Managing my self-worth, self-esteem, love of self, and self-acceptance has been the key and the core of everything. Acceptance, pure and simple acceptance of myself, my life, my lot in life, those people in my life, and even those I find hard to love, have given me peace.

I know it seems simple as I write this, but we would all do it in a heartbeat if it was that simple. It is a process that will continue until I take my final breath, as even during those final breaths, I am sure my journey of surrender will go to an even deeper level.

That's why I dedicate Part One of this book to the journey of mastering my emotions. Throughout each chapter, I talk about my experiences, how I have overcome them, and how I practice, even today, to manage life's highs and lows and ensure I remain at the top of my emotional game.

***

"I just want to be me," were the words that erupted from my mouth as I sat in my car crying out loud. Again, as I shrieked out the exact words, my throat now hurt. I was screaming so loudly. I didn't care who heard me. In fact, the rain pelted so hard on my parked car I doubted if anyone could. If they did, it didn't matter to me now.

This night nearly thirty years ago is what I describe as one of the low points in my life—not the lowest—however, one that was bad enough for me to declare within, "No more! Not one more day will I live like this."

I don't recall how long I remained in the car or what happened when I returned home, but I know that something had changed in me. It was a pivotal moment. At twenty-eight years of age, I had made a decision. Even though I was not sure of the direction I would take, I knew that remaining stuck and secretly suffering was no longer an option.

I decided to take ownership of my happiness that night. I decided to become unstuck, whatever that looked like.

From the outside looking in, no one knew about my internal anguish, even my parents. I was good at hiding it. One would think I had it all together. I was educated, self-employed, and always appeared to be happy and confident.

This was the mask I wore on the outside; however, deep down, I was just trudging through life and not being me, not pushing through the walls around me to feel fully alive, and keeping myself small. I figured this was my lot. I had made some decisions that were not great, and I now had to live with them. After all, what would everyone think?

But on this wintery night, sitting in my car looking out at the ocean, I said *no more* and decided to break free. Even though I had been a self-development junkie from the early age of sixteen, it was now time to do something about my situation. Taking action was quite different than simply reading another book and learning more about what *not* to do with my life. I knew it wouldn't be easy. However, this time, I knew for sure that something inside me had snapped, and I had finally made the long-awaited decision. If I wanted my life to change, I needed to change. I could not rely on anyone else to do this for me. I needed to change and do it for me.

Fast forward thirteen-plus years after that night in my car. Here I was again, on a cold winter's night, crying out in pain. Newly widowed, it was as if I had gone back in time and once again reached a crossroads in my life. Even though I had created a strong foundation and personal identity in my thirties and was settled in so many areas of my life, once again, I was in pain. I did not know who I was anymore or what I should do. I was stuck.

In those initial months after a major life adversity, you are in shock, walking around in a haze. However, once the haze dissipates and you are in about month three, you wake up in the dark reality of what just happened. For me, my husband had died. He was not coming back. His death was real. This was my life now, and I had no choice but to learn to live again.

But I don't know who I am anymore, I wrote in my journal. My life felt split in two. Half of me was gone. I felt as though I was living in a nearly empty shell. Nothing fit in my life, not even me.

Before Phil's death, I had a strong identity of being a spouse. I could call myself a wife. Even though we did not have children, I always held on to the hope that I would one day be a mom. So, I was Tanya, a mother in waiting, a mother-to-be. Then, in a matter of months, I was neither. What did that make me? Who was I now?

It was interesting that even the change of status from married to widowed was enough to throw me off—just one word. I disliked the word "widow" and refused to call myself one. I would not let anyone else refer to me as a widow, either. I chose to wear no longer black, as it reminded me of death and Phil's funeral, and I knew I did not want to be stuck there.

Even though I felt the darkness on the inside, I did not want it to show on the outside. I did not want people to label me, pity me, or put me in a box. I had spent my younger life doing that to myself, feeling different and believing I was not good enough, but now, I promised never to do that again.

I was fully aware that my confidence had taken a hit and that I felt fragile. I felt fearful of what my future would be like. I knew I had to make the same decision again to take control of my life and my happiness. I would not allow myself to fall into an abyss of darkness. Also, I knew that Phil would not have wanted me to do that, just as I would not have wanted it for him if we reversed the roles.

During those dark nights when the pain was at its greatest, the truth that was a part of me no longer wanted to live, and the thought of another forty years was daunting. During those times, I would hold on to the belief that there must be a greater plan for me.

My deep belief in the bigger picture enabled me to get out of bed every day to find meaning in my life, to find me again, and to live again.

Besides, my cat Fergus needed me, and on those days when I struggled with my identity, I held on to the fact that I was still a mom to this fur baby. Truthfully, this made me a 'somebody,' and it is safe to say that only Fergus got me through another day sometimes.

The other thing I knew with my heart was that I was a 'somebody' to God. Even though I felt He had put me through the wringer again, I still believed. I trusted God knew the big picture. He had a greater plan for my life that was well beyond my wildest imagination, and I believed He knew I was up to it.

Throughout this book, I write about my faith in God because it is a big part of my journey. Faith has always played a large role in my life and my recovery, and in a way, has formed who I am.

Now, this is my God, a God of my understanding, and if you, too, believe in God or you are searching for God, then that is great. It doesn't matter, and never has to me, who your God is, how you worship, or what name you give your God.

Every spiritual book tells me that God loves me, and I hold on to this during my dark moments. I believed, purely and simply as a child would, that God loved me and that I was worthy, which must mean there is a reason for me.

God's love for me and my cat's needs were reasons enough for me to decide to live and live fully. Rightly or wrongly, I wanted to make Phil proud. I wanted to be strong for all those people out there who were suffering because of his death.

Many people did not even know he was ill, and this was the way he wanted it. They learned of his illness the same day they learned of his death. Naturally, they were hurting, and I felt a responsibility to help everyone else find meaning even though I was still searching.

Everything begins with a decision, and our decisions form the quality of our lives. Are you procrastinating about making a decision, knowing that your choice would make a significant difference in your life if you made it?

Chapter: 2

Believing You Can

"How old are you," my boss asked. Immediately straightening my posture, I proudly responded, "Sixteen."

"How fast do you think you could get your driver's license," he continued. "I need you to get out on the road and drive when one of the other sales reps goes on extended leave."

Without thinking about how I would do it, my immediate response was, "I am on to it." I then turned and strutted out of his office like a woman on a mission because I was.

The only two times I had sat behind the steering wheel of a vehicle was when I was seven on a tractor while growing up on the farm. Then again, when I was about fourteen and out on a drive with my big brother Zel in his Jensen Healey sports car, he suddenly stopped at an intersection on quite a steep hill. He then got out of his car and instructed me to take the wheel and start driving. Needless to say, I appreciated his belief in me. Feeling like a grownup, I went home, learning how to drive at the same time.

So, of course, having the instruction from my boss to get my license at sixteen was quite a nudge, and without giving it another thought, the yes just popped out of my mouth. It also boosted my confidence that someone believed in me. Wanting to show him what I could do only drove me forward and gave me a strong reason to make it happen.

After ten weekly driving lessons from an instructor, I sat for my test and received my license on a Saturday morning. The following day, I went to my work colleague's home and collected the Mazda 323, which would be my company car for the next three months. I couldn't believe my luck!

Driving it home on that Sunday afternoon was the first time I was ever to be the sole occupant driving a car. I put on my positive pants, had someone follow me home, and told myself I could do this. The following day would be my true test when I headed into the central city for my first day at work.

I took on this role as a sales rep during a gap year before I commenced university. I planned to begin my studies for a Bachelor of Commerce Degree the following year. However, I was too young to begin, so I decided to take the year off to study and experience work life.

Some said I was mad. I thought I was brave. I didn't want to follow what everyone else was doing, which was to keep studying until you are accepted into university and then study some more. I had already been accepted, and I trusted that I would make up for whatever I missed out on during my gap year.

I knew I needed an education in life, plus my parents allowed it, only on the proviso that I commence university the following year.

My office was in the middle of the central business district of Auckland City. Early morning traffic was always heavy, and this would be my first time driving alone in rush hour traffic. Then, I had to pull into a car park for the very first time and park the car.

It was a lovely sunny morning, and I distinctly remember driving down Queen Street with my hands clenched at the wheel. There were cars behind me, in front of me, and going in the opposite direction on the other side. I was tense. I was scared, and I felt that everyone was looking at me. The voices in my head were starting to play their ugly tune, saying I wasn't good enough.

Then, just like that, something inside me switched. I remember it distinctly as I have always recalled this switch as being one of those pivotal moments in my life that showed me how quickly I could change how I felt about myself. Suddenly, I said out loud, "No one else knows this is the first time I am driving down one of the busiest roads in the city during peak hour traffic. No one knows that I only passed my driving test less than forty-eight hours ago. Only I know, and for now, I am going to pretend."

So, I loosened my grip on the steering wheel and relaxed. I reminded myself that everyone else who was driving around me wasn't focusing on me. Nobody knew I was only sixteen and scared at the wheel, so I decided to pretend I wasn't. Today, I am still a confident person behind the wheel.

My tense knuckles were no longer white, my shoulders relaxed as I confidently drove, and I felt a little cocky. This experience showed me that all I needed to do was believe that I was a good driver. I went that little bit further and pretended I was this important businesswoman driving her fancy car to her fancy office.

Every time the ugly voice in my head went off again, trying to tell me to be scared, I turned it around and believed the opposite. Even though I knew I was pretending, this strategy seemed so simple and worked. I didn't try to analyze it; I just kept driving like a boss.

What happened on that Monday morning drive in the Mazda 323 was one of my most valuable lessons. I am grateful to have learned so early in life that I could control my thoughts. Did I always remember to use it? No. Have I needed others to remind me of this in other ways and how to change how I feel? Yes. I have had to relearn this lesson repeatedly.

However, I have never forgotten that first time, and it is this first time that returns to me so quickly when I need to remind myself of how quickly I can escape from that stupid voice trying to drag me down.

That voice caused me to struggle, and I grew up. I never believed I was good enough, that I was different. So, to compensate, I decided that someday I was going to be someone who would help other people.

Yes, it was pretend. However, this fantasy was something I used and held on to when other stories would weigh me down. When I felt low as a teenager, I would go for long walks and daydream about making a difference in the world in the lives of others.

Fast forward twenty-four years. Here I was at forty, alone, feeling different again. It could have been so easy for me to fall into a place of suffering, feeling like a victim because of the hand that life had dealt me. Instead, I chose to do the opposite, just like I did when I sat in that Mazda 323.

Once again, between the bursts of grief, I would step into this persona of someone else who had the strength to carry anything asked of her and use this lesson to make a difference in the world and help change the lives of others. Perhaps, at times, it was a mask, and that was okay. It worked. The more I went into that state, the more I was able to believe that it was possible.

During those early months after Phil died, I began walking again and daydreaming. I listened to audiobooks during my walks. I have several favorite books on how to deal with life, and the two that I re-read or listened to were Viktor Frankl's *Man Search for Meaning* (2005), and the Book of Job in the Bible (*Life Application Bible*, 1988).

Frankl reminded me that no matter how bad your life is in the moment and how out of control you might feel, your mind is the one thing you have control over. I chose to hold on to the belief that despite the reality of my sorrow, I could create a new reality in my mind and create a bubble of peace, calm, and possibility.

The Book of Job reminded me that no matter how many times I got knocked down, my only choice was to get back up again. After all, what was the alternative? What was my alternative? During those walks, I developed a deep belief that I had what it took to get back up again and accomplish whatever I wanted to.

During my walks, I would always remind myself of that time in the kitchen when I felt God's presence in my heart, knowing that there was a reason for what I was going through, that He had His hand on the situation and me; and that in time, all would be revealed. It always made me feel special in God's eyes that He had a task for me during my lifetime and that He had called on me because He believed in me. This belief alone was enough for me to believe in myself.

Strengthening my belief in myself would help me rise and grow into this identity of Tanya, the woman who could handle anything. Just like when I was sixteen and believed I was a pro at driving a car, now at forty, I told myself that I could survive this too.

If you are going through something difficult right now, what will it take for you to change your belief from "I can't" to "I can, and I will?"

Chapter: 3

Knowing Your Worth

One of my most extraordinary experiences was being invited to the Crystal Cathedral in Garden Grove, California, to be interviewed by the late Dr. Robert Schuller. It was September 2009, and my first book, *Unplanned Journey,* was released earlier that year. This was the last of several television interviews during a whirlwind tour around the United States.

We filmed two church services, where I shared the content of my book and my journey of surrender and resilience. In between these services, Dr. Schuller and I had an amazing discussion in his office, talking about life. He was incredibly curious and supportive of me and asked many questions about my past journey and what I wanted for the rest of my life.

During our chat, he shared his beliefs with his friend, the famous author and Holocaust survivor Dr. Viktor Frankl. They believed that everything in life came back to our self-worth and self-acceptance. This was one of the deepest life-changing conversations I will always remember. It taught me that if ever I felt off about something, I knew the first place to look for the answer was within.

One of the stories my mother shared with me countless times was how as a three-year-old, when my parents would take me to a dance, I would always be the first one on the dance floor. No doubt, Mom dressed me up like a big white marshmallow, with a massive ribbon in my hair that looked like a helicopter propellor holding up my big mop of blonde curls.

The music would begin, and like always, I would be out there dancing, swirling around in my white dress without a care in the world. Clearly, at that age, I could feel free and dance, unconcerned about who was watching, what people were saying, or what they were thinking. I remember feeling such freedom for a long time during my youth.

Then life happens, and we grow and absorb what is happening around us. We listen to the words spoken the tone of the language used, and we understand it in our own way. We observe the actions of people, listen to our friends, watch the media, and slowly but surely, our own innocent, carefree interpretations of life are clouded over. We create our own model of the world—our own beliefs about who we are and who we are not.

We begin to build stories in our innocent minds of things that do not make sense. We listen closely to the words of others that are not true. However, for some reason, we believe them over ourselves. We then carry on with life, believing the story about ourselves and, worse still, continuing to find more evidence to prove the false story to be true.

This was my journey and why I needed to do something about it. In my twenties, I began to pray to God about my worth. Whilst I didn't fully understand it, or perhaps believe it, apparently God loved me and knew my worth. So, instead of questioning His judgment, I believed it was true.

During my daily prayer time, I began to ask God every day to help me feel how much He loved me. I used to say, Apparently, you do openly. *Please show me and help me to feel even a smidgen of how much you love me today. This doesn't come naturally to me, so please, Lord, help me out. Let me know and feel you, even though I may not fully understand your love.*

Every time I fully surrendered to God and asked for understanding during my prayer time, it worked, and soon, I believed Him. So, I kept praying.

Here I was again all these years later, as I sat in the reality of my grief and loneliness as a young widow, questioning my worth. It wasn't easy to recall all the personal development work I had done during the previous decades and all the people I had helped in my life. With my identity shaken and my sense of purpose gone, the loneliness took over. During some of those long, empty days and dark nights, I found it difficult to believe in my worth.

Loneliness can be a dangerous prerequisite to the decision-making process. Even though I knew what to do, the grief and loneliness at times clouded my decisions, and on several occasions, I made some not-so-good ones, which added to my self-doubt.

Thankfully, the fighter in me arose and decided to climb out of that abyss and to appreciate and feel gratitude for life, which meant maintaining belief in myself. Once again, every single day, often multiple times a day, I retreated to a place of silence and peace. I took time to breathe, journal, surrender, and once again talk to God until I felt grounded and worthy.

I would walk long distances because I knew how much the exercise would lift my spirits. As I walked, I prayed, listened to music or books, or simply went to my imaginary place of strength. Intellectually, I knew I was not worthless. However, when you have been dealt a tough hand and are vulnerable, you make unhealthy decisions. It can be so tempting to buy into the lie that you are a victim, making excuses and believing you are not enough.

As I began to rebuild my self-worth, I made sure my foundation was stronger, and what followed were better decisions about my life. I also added a few extras to my daily prayer about joy. I needed to know joy was possible, even in the presence of grief, and that I was worthy to feel it. I would say, *Lord, I do not know how to feel or even allow myself to feel joy. Please help me today.*

I used to chat to Phil. I knew he was happy in heaven. So, I used to ask him on my dark days to help me feel a smidgen of the joy he was feeling up there. When grief enveloped me, I knew not to stay in that state. Inviting and allowing joy into my life was a part of my journey to self-worth.

What is a quick and easy prayer or request that you can say to snap you from feeling worthless to feeling worthy and loveable?

Exercise: Remember when?

As you are reading this, you may not feel that great about yourself or even be able to say, *I am worthy*. I remember the first time I got asked to say those words during a therapy session. I could say the actual words; however, I didn't mean them at all.

A lot has changed since then. Now, I feel absolute peace, calm, and true self-acceptance. These gifts have grown and developed over the years, and whilst I am human, I still wobble at times. I know, without a doubt, that if I am troubled, the first place to look is within. Something has shaken my identity, and I need to be aware of what it did and change my response.

A helpful exercise I teach is to anchor yourself to a time in your life when you felt true peace within and unconditional acceptance of yourself simply because of who you were. You may respond with, "I have never felt this way." My advice is to take some time and think about your past. It might be only a short period of time, even five minutes. Do your best to remember that feeling.

Was it a time in your life when you felt fully aligned with a higher purpose? A time when you were doing something for the greater good or helping another person make a deep personal transformation? You gave of yourself unconditionally, and all you wanted to do was serve that other person for no other reason than serving them.

It may have been your child, and there may have been a time when you held your child and nothing else mattered. You felt content and at peace. There was no judgment from anyone, especially not from you.

It may be a time when you have already overcome extreme adversity, tragedy, or loss. The point is you overcame it. You already have this resilience inside of you; at times, it is simply about remembering.

Whenever it was, recall that moment and write it down if you must. Remember what it felt like, knowing that it was simple and real. There was nothing external bringing you this level of fulfillment and peace. It all came from within.

Imagine that you found a key to connect to yourself or something greater than yourself, and you felt a natural calm and deep knowing you were being your true authentic self. This is what I am asking you to recall and use that place, that state, as an anchor, somewhere for you to go when you need to reconnect with who you really are.

I experience those feelings when I help another human being prepare for their final act on earth and help them pass with grace and dignity. And I know those feelings in other areas of my work where I know lives are being impacted deeply. This small reminder always takes me out of that funk we can fall into and momentarily think we are not enough.

What evidence or memories do you have as a reminder to take you back to a place of certainty that you are worthy and enough?

Remembering it, writing about it, and holding on to this memory is what will ground you. It will be evidence to draw on if and when you feel as though you have lost who you are. Those memories will always be there within you; it is you.

Chapter: 4

Acceptance

In 1982, at the age of eighteen, I walked into my first twelve-step meeting. My sister-in-law, who knew of the issues I had with food and my body image, discovered an organization that could apparently help people who ate too much. Believing it was another diet club that would show me how to regain some control, I was all in. By the end of my first meeting, I was somewhat disappointed that I had not handed another diet plan to follow. It was, however, the beginning of something new.

Without question, during the years when I attended various twelve-step meetings, the life-long relationships I formed and the principles of the twelve-step program have played a big part in my life. Everything I learned at such an early age has been a big part of navigating through my later teenage years, my tumultuous twenties, and the life events that followed. Despite being raised in a faith-based home, the program was quite an eye-opener on how to let go and let God.

The most powerful lesson for me was to learn about acceptance, surrender to what is, and how to stop trying to fight it. I wanted to accept life as it was, to make meaning of my situation, and to focus on what was good instead of what was terrible. I taught myself the power of living in the now, the twenty-four hours I was in, and accepting my life as it is today.

It was also the beginning of my journey of accepting me. Instead of living in the shame of the past or fearing my future, just for today, one day at a time, I started liking myself.

During the early days, I thought it was all about food and my weight. I believed that I would be happy once I reached a specific number on the scale, and everything else would fix itself. Here's the thing: my weight was normal;

however, my thinking wasn't, and it took me a while to understand that.

When I eventually experienced periods of not overeating and came off the crazy diet/binge cycle, not a lot changed, and I still didn't feel good about myself. If anything, a part of me felt worse because everything I did not want to feel now stared back at me. Then, the cycle would start again.

It was not until my twenties that I was prepared to fully let go and accept that my behavior was not just about the food or my weight but so much more. I had to put a stop to repeating patterns that were clearly not working and begin a deep journey of acceptance and a decision to change. This meant finally dealing with those things that came up once I put the food down.

Throughout the decade that followed, I learned acceptance was the answer to everything in my life and that I would struggle to find peace without learning how to accept myself and my life as it was. Without peace, I would continue the search outside of myself for the solution to my problems, reaching for that new sparkling quick-fix scheme. By continuing to reach for a quick fix, the repair would be brief and only skin deep.

Learning the art of acceptance did not come overnight. I still need to remember to surrender daily. There is a part of me that still wants to be in control and try to make things happen, falling into the trap of frantically looking for the answers around me. It takes discipline to patiently be still, go within, and listen for divine timing. This is what has always worked for me. The trick is to do it every single day.

Acceptance helped me to come to a place of peace and calm during intense times of loss in my life. Each time the tsunami of grief would come and envelop me, I would remember those words, "Thy will be done," or even say out loud, "God, just for today, help me to accept what is."

Acceptance ultimately helped me through the years of not conceiving a child. Month after month I waited, building up my hope, only to be disappointed. I admit those highs and lows were tough in the beginning. However, each month each year, surrender and acceptance helped me through. After an eight-year rollercoaster and then Phil's diagnosis, I fully let go and understood. "Thy will be done," I said, as I listened to that feeling inside going, "Shh. Everything is as it should be."

Acceptance enabled me to do what I needed to do each time a friend or family member was diagnosed with cancer. I became known as the go-to person for comfort; hence, I needed to show up and support these people. The way I did it was to accept the reality of what I was facing and hold them on their journey. I was their strength. Slowly but surely, I learned how to accept, take ownership, and not allow fear to take over until Phil.

During Phil's diagnosis and illness, I had brief moments of acceptance. However, what accompanied the acceptance was unbearable grief because acceptance also meant he was going to die. I would not allow Phil to see my grief, not much anyway, but he knew why I cried at times.

It was the acceptance that enabled me to be present with Phil during his final hours. A deep surrender to God's will, so much so that it felt He was present with us that night. There was no room for tears or fear. The acceptance that followed his death was quite extraordinary.

It was as if I fell on my knees and surrendered my life fully into God's arms and accepted my fate. It did not mean there was an absence of grief, far from it. Eventually, it meant I was able to allow acceptance and grief to coexist and, over time, allow moments of joy in as well.

Acceptance was my answer and the most important thing to work on regularly. I finally realized, though, that acceptance was not something to work on; it was something to allow, to let be, to let go and surrender to the flow of life. Each time I found myself working on acceptance and my white knuckles would appear, it was an indicator that I was still trying to be in control and had to let go.

Interestingly, my journey of acceptance of the big events in my life paved the way for my ability to accept and eventually let go of the smaller stuff that took up so much of my head space—trying to control my food, my body size, other people's feelings, and even trying to fix everyone else. There was so much in my life I couldn't do a thing about, so I learned to let it go.

I had to define what acceptance meant to me. It wasn't about giving up, or submission, or doing nothing and expecting life to be handed to me on a silver platter. Whilst it meant letting go, it also meant taking ownership of my life, happiness, and decisions. No matter what hand life has dealt me or in the future, I will do my best not to run from it but rather own it and face it.

It wasn't easy, and it still isn't at times; however, every day, deciding to accept life on life's terms is a daily must. If it feels too hard, you do it one day at a time, then you get up the next day and repeat, and the next day, you repeat. Some days may start off well, but then you are triggered and find yourself falling into the abyss. Reset, call a friend, pray, meditate, do whatever it takes to know that all you must do is live through this one day. Just one day at a time, accepting my circumstances was always my path to peace.

Elizabeth Kubler Ross (1989) so famously writes about the five stages of grief: denial, anger, bargaining, depression, and the final stage is, acceptance. Some mentioned that my blind faith in God, trusting in His will for me, meant I was in denial. However, with all my heart, I would still call it acceptance. Sprinkled along the way for many years were also brief episodes of fear, anger, and a bit of bargaining with God before Phil died. Those times of acceptance made my journey more manageable.

Today, the world is amid a global pandemic, and we are all in some way grieving life as it once was. There is so much fear and loss affecting every single one of us. Once again, one day at a time, what enables me to be fully present during this event is acceptance. Acceptance of what is today will always see you through.

Chapter: 5

Feel the Feelings or Else They Follow You

So, it is six weeks after the flood, and today I am feeling brassed off, and I want to scream at the top of my lungs so that everyone can hear I am at the end of my tether. I have had enough of life lessons. I have had enough of being challenged and feeling I need to be strong and stoic in front of the world. Sometimes, I just want to fall apart and let it all out. I think I will.

I am angry that I couldn't have kids. I am angry that Phil died. I am angry that people I trusted have taken advantage of me and been unkind. I am angry now that I am finally happy with my lovely husband, Grant, in our new home, and we only got to enjoy it for six weeks before the house was no more.

Now my lovely new home has been turned into a construction site. Dust layers everything. We are living in limbo, out of a suitcase, and now, to top it all off, Fergus has died.

This was one of my real-time rant journal entries after our new home flooded in the middle of 2017. A freak plumbing accident happened during the middle of the night, and for five hours, approximately thirty-five tonnes of water gushed through the house as we lay sleeping.

What we originally thought was going to be a drying-out exercise turned into a six-month, incredibly stressful period of rebuilding the house. This was then followed by my elderly parents showing signs of declining dementia, and then my cat of sixteen years, Fergus, suddenly died.

What pained me the most was that this was a new beginning for me, for us, and just as I was feeling true joy again, it was taken away. It would have been the perfect opportunity for me to fall into a place of feeling like a victim. Once again, life took it all away just when I allowed myself to move forward.

I had to dig deep and use every resource to rise above the negativity that brewed inside me. Once again, I had to acknowledge what had happened, accept it, and trust that God would bring good amid this terrible event. Somehow, someday, He would reveal it to me.

I had to step into that strong identity of Tanya, the resilient woman who believed in herself and who knew that this, too, would pass. I had everything within me to overcome the situation. I just had to get up, look up, say thank you, face it, feel it all, and get on with life.

Once upon a time, the stress would have been too much. I would have binged-eaten my way through something like this. Not anymore, though. Picking up food and squashing my feelings were no longer an option: the anger, the frustration, the grief. I had to go back to basics and feel the anger, the frustration, and the grief before I could accept it.

After learning to journal at fifteen and see a therapist at sixteen, I walked into my first twelve-step meeting at the age of eighteen. That's where I began the deep journey of not using food to cover up my feelings.

In each following decade, I explored deeper, found the right mentors at the right time, and committed to stop running from life and my feelings, no matter how bad it felt. As a result of this decision to say yes to the feelings, the fear of feeling them slowly dissipated. As a result, Tanya, the little girl, calmed down, and Tanya, the woman, began to emerge. This was how I got through the flood and many of the other setbacks in recent years. Tanya, the resilient woman, showed up. I was determined not to let this event knock me back.

I had created a lot of certainty around my identity as Tanya, the strong woman. I knew that no matter what came up for me, I could handle it. My fifties were empowering as I allowed all my feelings to surface. I faced them, made peace with them if I had to, and allowed them to pass through me. After all, what was my alternative?

If you choose to soothe yourself when you are uncomfortable, whether it be with food, alcohol, or even shopping, nothing changes, and the original problem is still there. In fact, you usually create another problem, as you are either drunk, bloated, broke, or smothered in remorse.

The first time you get through a day without soothing or using or running when you so wanted to is simply amazing! You wake up the following day feeling so clearheaded, even though the night before, all you wanted to do was run from the pain. Something inside you chose not to succumb to temptation. What you realize the following morning is that you survived the ordeal.

My journaling has been and continues to be one of the most powerful ways to process my feelings as they arise. It can be scary to face your feelings. However, it is not as bad as some of the self-destructive things you do to avoid them.

Physical exercise, which I will write more about later, was also a big part of my journey to unlocking my potential. Yes, at times, I overdid the exercise. However, it was better than the sluggish alternative. Soon, I found balance. I loved my early morning walks because, during this time, I talked the most to God, prayed, cried, and allowed myself to feel what I needed to.

One of the major turning points for me was to realize that life did not have to be either black or white. There was a healthy grey area in between. It was okay to laugh and cry at the same time. I welcomed all my feelings and allowed those around me to see the real me.

It was a pivotal moment to allow myself to be happy again. I had cried enough, and finally, I acknowledged that I deserved to live again, to laugh again, and to even love again, without the ever-present survivor's guilt hovering overhead. I allowed the grief, but I also began to allow the joy, and then, I allowed the joy and grief to coexist.

Feelings are a funny old thing. We run from them for so long, especially grief and sadness, which I cover more extensively in Part Two of this book. This is what I know to be true. If we allow ourselves to feel them, we realize that feeling them is not that bad after all.

What is one or more feelings you find yourself running from? Would you like to have the courage to look them straight in the eye and say, "I own you!"

Chapter: 6

Intuition – Emotional Mastery

Pavica Unkovich, born Pavica Samic, in a small village called Opuzen in the former Yugoslavia, would have to be one of the most non-compliant, stubborn, rest-home residents that ever existed. Don't get me wrong. I am not praising her naughty behavior. I admire her stubbornness, resilience, and belief that no one was better than her, that no one knew better than her, and that no one could tell her what to do.

Last year, at eighty-nine, she broke her hip badly, along with some vertebra and her pelvis. This was the end, we thought, but no, she told me she wasn't going to die because the world would be "shit" without her. Truth, those were her words, albeit slightly driven by dementia, but that was my mom.

Watching her tenacity and recovery during these past months has ignited a new level of respect for my mama. I have been reflecting on her life, what she has endured, and the lesson on resilience she taught me by her example.

One sentence my mother would often say to me was, "Tanya, nobody is better than you." The other one she would repeat was, "Tanya, trust yourself. You know you better than anyone else." When she wanted to get her own way, she added, "Only your mama knows better."

Whilst I tried to ignore that add-on piece about her knowing better than me, there is no doubt about it. My mother had a strong intuition and always knew more than she led us to believe, and even at eighty-nine, with dementia, she still does.

As frustrating as these past years have been with her decline, I quietly love that part of her, that strong intuitive part of her that she kept buried for so much of her life, now, at times, wishing she hadn't.

I often wondered why she repeated those instructions to me so much in my life. "Tanya, *no one* is better than you, and *no one* knows you better than you." Perhaps she saw how fragile her wee girl was growing up. Perhaps she understood me better than I thought she did. Maybe those times when I felt she was incredibly hard on me; she saw my weaknesses and lack of boundaries and was trying to protect me.

She was right. Growing up, I didn't understand boundaries, I didn't trust my inner voice or intuition, and as a result, I made some choices that did not serve me well and completely changed the trajectory of my life.

Here I was again, at forty, newly widowed, and despite having all those years of personal development and therapy and even studying to be a therapist, my foundation had been completely shaken. I was broken. I didn't quite trust myself or the decisions I made.

It is amazing how grief can rattle your foundation and identity. I felt vulnerable and afraid, which paved the way for the same insecurities to return. My mother knew I was deeply shaken. Those were the times when I needed to listen to my mother's mantra, and whilst I did listen to her, I was selective in when I applied it.

During these vulnerable times after a major life event, it is quite easy to turn to others and ask their opinions on what you should do. Many are also there, freely offering their advice. You begin to ignore your inner voice, the one that is screaming at you, as you listen to the quiet and sometimes calculated voices of others.

Here are the words of my mother: "Nobody is better than you, and you know more about yourself than anyone else. Listen to that inner voice, that whisper from God, your intuition. That first initial feeling you have about anything is usually spot on."

Every one of my experiences was a valuable lesson. Even the worst of betrayals and attempts to control me were lessons and reminders I needed. Without them, in recent years, I would not have delved so deeply into believing in myself and listening and trusting that inner voice.

These lessons reminded me of the importance of stopping to listen to the noise around me. I needed to tune out the toxic words of other people and instead tune into my frequency. This was where I would find the peace to listen, find the clarity I was searching for, and finally learn how to make and trust my own decisions again.

It did, however, mean letting go of some people in my life. It meant letting go of the fear of losing some people I once thought I needed and remembering the alternative was to lose myself if I continued to listen to them.

One of my favorite sayings is that when I keep saying yes to everyone else, then I am possibly saying no to me. Part of this process of trusting yourself and following your intuition is also having the courage to finally say no to some people. Being true to yourself may mean exploring new territory. It's important to establish healthy boundaries.

When I reflect on all the big decisions I have made in my life, the great ones, I made them all quickly by following my intuition. My new attitude affected relationships, buying property, and professional choices. I decided without running around asking for everyone else's opinion. They were big and bold decisions. I took a leap of faith, and the safety net always appeared.

Those decisions I made in the state of a fearful and doubtful little girl were never good! Listen to the voice of the Holy Spirit within you, and He will guide you in the way you should go.

The mentors I valued most were not the ones who felt the need to tell me what to do but rather those who encouraged me to listen to my God-given intuition. I invite you to do the same.

Chapter: 7

Forgiveness

Releasing Yourself to Shine

I distinctly remember the day when my local priest and father figure, Monsignor Cronin, gave me a right telling off. I was in full-blown victim mode and dining out big time on all the reasons why I couldn't forgive myself. Why? Because I should have known better. How could I have made such a big mistake; it is not like me to be so naïve.

Why did I not walk away when my instinct screamed at me to walk away? Why did I trust those people? Did I have such low self-worth to have settled, to have believed, to have continued to tolerate toxic relationships? Those were some of the bashings I gave myself, not only for the mistakes I made after Phil passed away, but also for the mistakes I made as far back as I was a teenager.

"What makes you so special that God chooses to single you out and not forgive you?" Monsignor asked. "If He has released you of these burdens you are carrying, what makes you so different that you are unable to forgive yourself?" Ugh. That went straight to my gut.

His stern words broke the strings on my violin, and as hard as it was to hear, it was true. Unless I forgave myself and others, I would not be free. This conversation snapped me out of my pity party, and if ever I am tempted to indulge in victimhood again, I remember our talk that day.

Holding on to anger, resentment, ill feelings, blame, or shame toward others or myself stops me from living. It stops me from allowing myself to move forward, to feel joy. It keeps me stuck.

Resentment and lack of forgiveness allow someone to live in your head rent-free, and I hate to think how many precious hours I have wasted feeling this way. I cannot think of how many food binges I had because of resentment or anger. Sometimes, even the things that might happen, the "what ifs" still live in my head.

No amount of excess food or alcohol or ranting in your head will show them how much they have hurt you. Putting it simply, holding on to negative emotions is harmful to you, toxic in fact. You are the one who continues to hurt you if you don't let go.

There is no scale to forgiveness. Forgiveness is forgiveness, and it is essential. Decide to forgive fully. No matter how big the grievance is, no matter who has hurt you, you somehow need to forgive.

Forgive for your sake. It is a decision. Do an honest inventory on your part of the situation, take ownership of what you've done, and do whatever you need to forgive sooner rather than later. Then move on. The risk of not letting go, of not forgiving others and yourself, is that you continue to be held back from fully living emotionally, physically, spiritually, and possibly even professionally.

There have been a few people in my life whom I have had to forgive. Truthfully, there were many I did not want to forgive. It wasn't easy. Why did I hang on to my anger and hurt for so long? For some reason, it must have been serving me. Perhaps it was my excuse for not being happy. It was their fault. Perhaps it was why I kept overeating. I binged because of what they did to me, called me fat when I was younger or spoke against me publicly.

We could all come up with many valid reasons to hold on to resentment; however, all you need to do is be ready and willing to be free of it. Let it go for your peace of mind. They probably have no idea you still feel that way toward them, and they are blissfully moving through life.

Forgiveness does not change the past, but it does change the future. So, it came back to the question of, will I allow myself to be happy, to be free, to allow joy - will I allow myself a happy future? It was necessary to be prepared to let go of what may have been a not-so-happy past.

When I resist the willingness to let something go or to forgive, I ask myself some questions. "So, Tanya, how much time do you think you spend each day thinking about this issue? How much of your emotional energy is consumed by adrenaline? How does it affect the other person by constantly thinking about them? Do they even know your resentment takes up so much of your precious time? How else would you like to spend this time if you freed yourself from harboring such resentment? So, is there any reason, Tanya, why you still want to hang on to this?"

Sometimes, we need to dig deep and be willing to forgive others. Sometimes, we need to pray for the willingness to forgive them. Sometimes, we need to pray for them. Many I know would rather have their teeth pulled than be praying for someone who has harmed them. Imagine how you would feel if that person had something terrible happen to them, i.e., the death of a child, a terminal illness, or a debilitating accident. Always remember that no matter how big the grievance is, it is about releasing you from the chains in your own mind.

If you are still resisting forgiveness, let me try one more thing to demonstrate the importance of forgiving yourself and being free.

Fast forward thirty or forty years, when you are in your twilight years, and ask yourself, "Why did I use up my precious energy by being so hard on myself? Why didn't I just forgive myself, let it go, and allow myself to be free? Holding on to this self-punishment has held me back for most of my life. I could have been so much more productive. I could have contributed to humanity on a much deeper level. I could have shown up more fully in my relationships. I could have felt so much better about myself. Why did I do this to myself? Why did I lose all of those precious years?"

What needs to happen to fully let go of whatever you are hanging on to? What needs to happen for you to free yourself once and for all? When will you do it?

Chapter: 8

Own It

One of the best decisions I ever made was to take ownership of my happiness. This was a big factor in my journey to emotional mastery. Did this mean that joy showed up daily and that life was easy once this decision was made? Of course not. Much of what happens in life, the people around me, and what they do and say are out of my control.

I took responsibility for what I had control over: my mind, my thoughts, and which ones I allowed in. Which thoughts I fed and which thoughts I discarded. What I chose to focus on, and what I chose to let go.

I took responsibility for the meaning I placed on what was happening at the moment, what someone said and did, and how I responded to all of the above. I took responsibility for what came out of my mouth when I responded, the words I used, and the language and tone I used. Most importantly, I took ownership of monitoring my intention in my response.

My identity as Tanya, the strong, resilient woman who practiced what she preached, has developed over the decades and continues to grow. I grew from an insecure little girl who, whilst she was an extrovert and loud at times, still covered up the pain inside and the belief that she was flawed at the core.

It was critical that each day, I fed, nurtured, and strengthened my identity as Tanya, the woman who took ownership of my behavior, life, feelings, and how I showed up in the world, personally and professionally.

Some might say I can appear a bit tough; however, at times, I need to be. Maintaining healthy boundaries has been necessary for me to ensure I continue to do what I do and, serve those who need to and take responsibility for their own lives.

Mentoring means leading others to step out of their brown puddle of mud, wipe themselves down, and humbly take responsibility for their actions as they bravely decide to move forward and do things differently.

Each day is a gift and our opportunity to do better. It doesn't come easy, and motivation is not always present, which is why discipline needs to be. Whilst we can have the best mentors in the world, everything is up to us and the decisions we make in our lives. You will reap the benefits when you decide yes to you and yes to life. If you are still sitting on the fence, you haven't owned your life and happiness yet.

What needs to happen for you to fully "own" and say "yes" to life?

I invite you to make the decision today to make your emotional well-being a daily must and watch the remainder of your life follow.

Part II

• The Grief Journey •

Chapter: 9

The Lessons on Loss Begin

I can still recall the look on my father's face when he collected us from school that day. It was October 1971, the brightest of days. The image I have is of my father opening the car door as he collected us early from school that day. I knew something was wrong, for us not to be making the regular bus ride to our country home. He was smartly dressed, not in his usual farm attire, and there were no smiles for us. My father's strong, masculine face looked broken, and that made me feel incredibly sad.

He didn't take us home. My father did not want us to see, when we got off the bus, that our cottage on the hill was no longer there. He wanted to be the one to tell us that our home had burned to the ground, and all that was left was a cloud of black smoke hovering in the clear afternoon sky.

We went to a family friend's home, where my mom was sitting at their kitchen table, crying. I was only seven years old and couldn't imagine what my parents endured that afternoon as they watched their home—and most of their possessions—burn to the ground like paper.

What I did feel that day, sitting with her, was extreme sadness. I am not sure if it was mine or hers, but it hurt me so badly. This was my first experience of that feeling called grief.

The griefs that followed—the infertility, Phil's death, my parents' ill health, the loss of our home, Fergus dying—have all been part of the tapestry of my life that built resilience, so that I could then live out my ultimate purpose. I believe with every fibre of my being; it was all part of the bigger picture.

As they say, grief is the price you pay for love, and because we all yearn for love and connection, grief becomes a part of life. One of my past mentors shared with me that life is a series of griefs, separated by joy. I suppose it is about how we handle the loss in our lives, which ultimately determines how we embrace the joy when it shows up.

I can write in hindsight that my losses have given me an appreciation for life. Every single event has changed me for the better and enabled me to contribute to the world on a deeper level. Without them, I'm not sure I would have found my true purpose.

Whilst you are grieving, you do not see joy or feel it, and a part of you might be wanting to slap me right now if you could. I felt that way too—especially when one kept following the other. Each time I was faced with grief, it would bring back the memory, and sometimes tears, of my previous losses. This is common; we cannot help but be triggered again.

When my cat Fergus died, I cried every single day for three weeks—not only for him, but for everything else that he reminded me of during our sixteen years together. The answer is, and always will be: feel your emotions and allow everything to come out. Do not suppress your pain—feel it. You do not want it to accumulate like a clogged drainpipe that stops you from living. Just recently, I had a big cry, and once it was done, it was done. I recognised the trigger, allowed it, felt it, and eventually—and rather quickly—it passed.

Many times, people do not realise that what has been triggered is past grief. Instead, they focus on the anger that is present. They focus on the fact they just don't have the willpower to stop overeating, or they focus on whatever else is sitting on the surface. Soon enough, you may discover that the true emotion is grief.

As inviting as it can be, do not let these episodes take you into a place of isolation or self-destructive comfort. How easy it would be to dine out on our pain and suffering, to use it as an excuse for not rising—and instead, focusing on what is bad. The alternative is to turn your attitude around and focus on what you still have—how you can use this event in your life to somehow contribute to mankind.

We have a choice. We can choose to suffer, or we can choose to live. I invite you to choose life.

Chapter: 10

When Fear Knocks on Your Door, Send Faith to Answer It

My first experience of someone close to me being diagnosed with cancer was in 1997, when a cousin, at forty, was given the news that his cancer was terminal. Despite the sorrow, it was also a time of experiencing the power of unity in helping someone face their final act. The following year, the experience hit closer to home when my father was diagnosed with bowel cancer. This time, I was scared, and what was worse, I also saw the fear in my father's eyes. Once again, we felt the power in numbers, of coming together to support, pray, and face the fear head-on.

During the next five years, we were surrounded by an extraordinary number of friends and family facing life-threatening illnesses. Some survived; many did not. It was a very intense lesson on coping with grief, loss, and fear. However, also the power of faith, acceptance, and people uniting in prayer.

With each experience, the fear would lessen to the point where eventually, nothing shocked me. In 2003, when my mother was diagnosed with breast cancer, I had a deep belief that this was just a small glitch in her life. We would repeat the pattern of prayer and faith, and eventually, all would be well—and she was.

The following year, I was not so brave when Phil received his diagnosis. During the early stages, I was paralysed by fear, and no matter how much I prayed, believed, and tried to change my thoughts, the fear rarely left me. This time, something inside me knew that it was not going to be a small glitch. I knew that our lives had and would forever change; hence, my dance with fear was an ongoing one right up until his final day. It was only then, during his final hours, that fear stepped aside and acceptance took over.

The number of friends and family who continued to be diagnosed with cancer over the next few years bordered on weird. I became the go-to person where people would come for support, prayer, or spiritual guidance as they grieved, plus tried to navigate this suffocating feeling of fear.

This work soon became something I loved and still do. Walking beside someone who is facing the final stage of their life and helping that person come to a place of fearless peace and calm as they transition during this most pivotal time is a privilege. It is the most rewarding work I have ever done and continue to do.

Over the years, I discovered that choosing faith over fear was my only alternative—to be able to come to a place of acceptance very quickly and say, "Whatever He wants." Even when my dad, in his early eighties, was told that he not only had a recurrence of bowel cancer, but also lung cancer, I remained calm and was able to be there for him. I was no longer frozen by fear, yet I still remained present with grief.

One thing I did have to consciously stop thinking was that one day I, too, would get cancer. After all, it was clearly in my gene pool, so the thoughts were most definitely there. I knew I had to flatten them once and for all. Once again, I surrendered to the flow of life and took care of my health on every level. I couldn't let fear of the future overwhelm me and steal the joy of the present moment.

The more I deepened my spiritual path, the more I was able to release this fear and trust that life would unfold for me as it was meant to. The emotion you feed is the one that will grow, so I learned to feed my faith and starve the fear.

Is there an area in your life where fear is taking over? What needs to happen for you to replace this fear with faith, strength, and resilience? It begins with a choice.

Chapter: 11

Caring for the Caregiver

Never underestimate the power of adrenaline when you are the caregiver. You feel like a machine, physically and emotionally charged to do whatever it takes to help the person who is unwell. You must, right? How unfair is it that they are sick, and you are fully healthy? Why was it that they were given this cross to carry and you have a healthy, functioning body? It is very easy to feel you need to give your all to the other person—every ounce of energy that is in your body—without leaving any in reserve for you. If you take a moment to rest, then guilt, along with all the other feelings, comes knocking at your door. When it does, then I invite you not to answer the door. There is no room for guilt when you are a caregiver.

Probably the greatest comfort when we are first faced with such life-changing news is to be surrounded by your closest family and friends. Not many, just those few who know you well and will help carry you when you are unable to function properly. I also had an outstanding counsellor who helped me tremendously. Having others around during those initial days helps when you voice your fears, get them out in the open, and not allow them to fully envelop you.

It is during this time you allow your support network to help you in even the most basic of human needs. As a caregiver, you put all your energy into the person who is unwell, and it is very easy to find yourself not caring for yourself. Make your own self-care a must, or else soon you will not have the physical or emotional strength to care for your significant other. When illness strikes, the entire family unit is affected in various ways. We all cope differently. We all have different solutions on which path to take and how. Ultimately, whether we like it or not, the person who is unwell is the one who knows how they want to play out their final act.

It is not a time to be forceful. It is a time to come together and support each other in the best way possible, especially when time is limited.

It is not a time to carry guilt for what you did or didn't do, or what you are unable to do. There comes a time when no matter how stoic you want to be, as a caregiver you must accept help from others.

I know you want to spend every waking moment with your loved one, but even a few short hours of good sleep will make those hours afterward so much more valuable. You will have the energy to be present and fully experience that precious time.

As a caregiver, never apologise for your swaying emotions. No one prepares you for what is involved on this journey. I sought help very soon after Phil's diagnosis and continued with professional support for many years after his passing. I also relied on a network of close and trusted friends during this time, and, of course, I had an extended spiritual family at my church.

The reality of what has happened usually kicks you in the stomach hard after several months, when everyone else begins to return to their normal lives.

This is a time when you don't know what normal is anymore, so reach out to whomever you must to assist you during this time. No matter how resilient you feel you are, it is from my own experience that I say, allow yourself to fall into the arms of others when you need to. Let them comfort you.

Chapter: 12

Keep Living Even When You Are Grieving

Here is the truth. You never quite know what life is going to bring. Never in a million years did I think that I would be widowed at the age of forty, especially since we lived such a comparatively healthy lifestyle. Nor did I ever think that I would not be blessed with my biggest dream of having my own children.

What these two blows have taught me **is** that if you keep waiting for something to happen in your life, then chances are you could be waiting a long time. This was what I so often used to do. Wait for the baby or wait for this or that, then none of my dreams ever came true.

Being ready to bring a child into the world, and the excitement and preparation for it, is one of life's greatest gifts. When you try for eight years and nothing happens, then not so much. It becomes a chore, heartbreak, and an obsessive project if you allow it to. Whilst it is not an illness, the project can feel like one, and if not kept in check, **it** can eventually make you emotionally ill as it did for me.

The reason I share this story is not only for the many couples out there who are facing the same dilemma, but for anyone who is putting their life on hold waiting for "something" to happen or waiting for a certain result before you allow yourself to live your life.

We were not born to wait around, yet I waited for many years to conceive. I adjusted my professional life, my health, exercise, diet, and daily routines for this miracle to happen. In hindsight, I can now look back and say that I wish I hadn't. However, at that time, my desire to be a mother was so strong I was prepared to give up a lot to help make this happen.

I wasn't happy, and I am sure my unhappiness didn't help in the whole conception process. I was always waiting and grieving. I stopped myself from doing many things, which I now regret, as life took a very different turn.

In hindsight, had I known what would ultimately happen at age forty, then I would not have spent those eight precious years not living whilst waiting for something to happen. I would have lived more, travelled more, and not waited. When you are not living, then a part of you is dying, and whilst I cannot turn back time, I can most certainly make the decision to live each day—**today**, the one I am in—to the fullest.

The truth is, each day when we open our eyes, we should be excited for the new day, one we have never seen before, one we have never experienced before.

My message to you and to my younger self is, don't wait for anything (or anyone) before you allow yourself to live and be happy. Whether it is a child, a relationship, your ideal weight, a certain amount of money in the bank—whatever it is you are waiting for, then stop it.

Everything will get done; everything will be as it is meant to be. Meanwhile, live now, as life, as I discovered, could change in a heartbeat.

Chapter: 13

Honour Thy Mother and Father

During my early teens, when I was going through a particularly low patch, it was suggested by one of my best friends that I go and speak to this elderly couple who might be able to assist me in some way. From my teenage perspective, this couple was so old they were nearly dead, and I did wonder how on earth they could help me. Still, I trusted my friend and took her advice.

To this day, even as I type, I can remember the room I was in with them both, and them waving goodbye to me as I drove away. I will never forget the comfort I felt during those few hours I was with them, as they counselled me and prayed for me. Despite my reservations, it was this elderly couple, with all their years of wisdom, who made a significant difference in my life on that day.

Whilst now much of the conversation has left me, I do remember a story they told me on the importance of absolute honesty and good intention, and how, no matter what, practicing these in your life would always come back and reward you in the most amazing ways. They shared with me their own stories, and this, I can say, has been true in my life also.

What I have is a vivid recollection of when the elderly man asked a question of me. "Are you at peace with your parents?" Whilst there was nothing of significance at that time to share apart from usual teenage grumbles, the question made me think, and the subsequent conversation on the importance of honouring my parents has had a profound effect on the remainder of my life.

I have never forgotten what this elderly man said to me. "No matter what, honour your mother and father." He went on to elaborate that if we did not feel at peace in our hearts toward our parents, it would be very difficult to find that peace with ourselves.

The reason this conversation stuck with me at such an early age was because of the way they delivered the message to me. It was not forceful or authoritative, it was gentle, compassionate, and delivered with absolute certainty of its truth. It was so profound that, as a teenager, I heard them and never, ever forgot that piece of advice. The conversation with this couple has been invaluable in my own journey toward finding peace within and sharing this powerful story with others.

So how did this conversation impact my life? It has always remained tucked away in the back of my mind, and during difficult moments, at times when my patience was worn thin, these words would resurface. Perhaps not immediately, but eventually, they would. I discovered that, for me, harmony with my parents, and others as well, even if it was only in my own mind at times, was vital if I wanted to live a peaceful life.

It enabled me to get through those difficult times with my parents—we all have them—and to remember that we all have our failings. It would always remind me of who they were, where they came from, what they had lived through, and what they had learned as coping mechanisms in this life.

It taught me to show compassion, not to judge, and, when I did, then to eventually come back to a place of understanding, still maintaining strong, healthy boundaries. This incredible conversation enabled me to remember what I loved about my parents' souls and to detach from behaviours that I could not accept or change. I was able to see their suffering, to forgive and make amends when necessary, and to know and accept that sometimes the best we can do is simply love and support our parents. We cannot take away their pain or their history, we can simply honour what we know to be true—that they are, and always will be, my mother and father.

Chapter: 14

Appreciating the Lessons Learned

My father's resilience never ceases to amaze me. At eighty-nine, he is an outstanding example when it comes to the power of having a positive mindset over his health. He has faced cancer four times in his life, not to mention other life-changing events, and still his mind is focused on nothing apart from when the next best day is to go fishing.

Despite the fear I saw in his eyes all those years ago during his first cancer diagnosis, it was he who gave me incredible strength at that time. As I cried, he told me that this was not going to beat him, and he always held on to that belief. Within twelve hours of his surgery, he was waking the nurses in the middle of the night to turn on his television set so he could watch the World Cup soccer matches which were being played on the other side of the world.

During his second bowel cancer diagnosis, when he was eighty-four, they discovered that he also had lung cancer. Two cancers at the same time meant two separate surgeries, six weeks apart. Despite looking like he had been attacked by a shark, one month later he was out fishing. He did, however, mention it was difficult to bring in some of the big fish after his lung surgery!

He lives each day knowing that one day soon, one will be his last, which makes me ask the question: why do we have to wait until we are elderly or faced with life-threatening illnesses before we decide to live our lives with courage?

Then there is my mother, who at nearly ninety, has a body so worn, a mind so tired, and a life that we would not want to endure for a week, let alone a lifetime, yet still believes that she is the only one who can hold the family and the world together.

The poverty and horrendous experiences they experienced and witnessed during their upbringing in Communist Yugoslavia during the Second World War, and everything else attached to it, makes our difficulties in today's world seem like the size of a pinhead.

Which is why, no matter how difficult times have been, I reframe my grief and frustrations and always come back to my parents' example of resilience and hard work. I remember to honour my mother and father.

We think we have it hard because we are currently living in a pandemic. I suspect it has nothing on what the generation before us used to live with.

One of the greatest healing exercises I did was to document all the lessons learned from my parents, even the hard ones. During this process, whilst writing down even those difficult lessons and painful experiences, I was able to turn it around and see the gift in each of them.

When I struggled to find a gift amongst the pain, then I looked harder, and I could usually find one. When I still struggled to see the good, then it enabled me to see that at least I had the gift of contrast, meaning I was able to see another way through and live my life differently.

It was never difficult to reframe my thoughts, even the tough lessons from my parents, and always come back to that place of honouring my mother and father, and ultimately, accept that peace.

Chapter: 15

The Cycle of Life – Caring for Aging Parents

Once again, grief revisits as you watch your parents age, becoming frail, especially when once they were physically and emotionally strong individuals. Watching their bodies change from being muscular and fit, to weak and losing the tone and strength they once had, was difficult. They used to cook magnificent meals, but now they did not have the strength to lift the pot, or even forgot that the oven was on with nothing in it.

This is life, and if there is one lesson to learn from it, is to appreciate what we have when it is here: our parents, our family, our friends. Life passes quickly, and everything can change in an instant. We never know what each day will bring, or when we will receive the last phone call or hug.

This is certainly something in my own mind when I visit with them. Each time I speak to them or see them, I ask myself: How was the visit? How did the conversation end? It is quite a privilege to walk beside your parents as they age or receive the diagnosis that they are terminally ill. As they are now living and playing out their final act, it is important to let them transition peacefully, with dignity, but also for me to remain at peace when they go.

I am the first to say it is not an easy journey when difficulties arise, and they do. When it came to a point where our aging parents became difficult and resistant to what we all knew was best for them, to restore my own peace of mind, I let go. I simply prayed and said to God, "This is actually beyond me. There seems to be no clear solution that either party will accept or agree to, and there is nothing more I can do." These are common issues children or family must face.

My regular prayer was, "Please God, I ask for a solution." I knew that both of my parents were very proud and that both had an element of non-acceptance of this stage of their lives. Forcing it upon them was not going to work.

Often, stepping away from the situation and letting go will quieten heightened emotions and the decisions that have to be made. You manage it with a different frame of mind. Letting go completely would feel like the more peaceful solution.

No longer was I trying to fix my parents or their emotional state. I couldn't, and despite trying it many times, it never worked. Yet, I kept trying, until I no longer did. Instead, I became like a coach standing on the sideline. I kept an eye on things and respected their wishes.

When your parents need you, then return to the field and do what you need to. Instead of grief and frustration over something I could not control, I reframed the situation. It was now replaced with a new attitude, with three words playing in my mind: patience, mercy, and compassion. So long as I focused on these three states whenever I was dealing with my parents, their situation, their emotions, their grief, and frustration, then I was able to remain in a far greater state of peace myself.

Each day, I reminded myself that I had handed them over to God. There was only so much I could do now. To be strong meant being strong for myself first, and only then could I be strong during my visits with my parents. On some level, I had to imagine they were in a movie, and I was watching this movie, not directing it, but watching it.

To be able to truly honour my mother and father during such a difficult time, I had to also honour myself and my own state of mind. No matter what my parents or other family members were feeling, I owed it to myself to remain calm and continuously remind myself that I could not rescue anyone. Eventually, in the end, everything worked out as it was meant to.

Chapter: 16

Real-Time Grief as You Watch Your Parents Fade Away

This week, the grief is with me daily. Sometimes it stays with me all day, then there is a reprieve when I go to sleep at night, but it returns when my eyes open again. Keeping busy helped; however, that dull sadness remained.

No matter what has been said up until this time, the angry words and foolish actions, it is all forgotten as I sit with the reality that once my mother's light is extinguished, she is gone from this earth.

There will be no more daily phone calls, no more pain-in-the-butt conversations with her. Little did I know what was happening behind the scenes because she hid her pain, her confusion, and the changes in her own body.

I wrote this piece in my diary when it was confirmed that Mom had dementia. If only I had known this during those frustrating conversations when she was so angry; it felt as though I was speaking to someone whom I had never met before.

What followed were a couple of very difficult years with both parents, and from what I have heard since, many people go through the same ordeal, especially when dementia is part of the equation.

Watching a parent fade away is difficult at the best of times. Watching a parent fade away when you know they haven't fully lived is heart-wrenching. Especially when you know you have spent much of your life trying to make their life better, feeling sadness watching them in their suffering. Feeling frustration, anger, and hurt when you tried to make their life better, but for some reason, they chose suffering. Suffering was a more familiar emotion than joy.

Now as I watch both of my parents fade away, I cannot help but feel the grief of their loss, even though they are still with me. What pains me the most is watching my mother. This woman who gave her life for her children. A beautiful woman, who was intelligent and capable. She was young, fell madly in love, married young, and so wanted a child, and then there were four.

She lived for her children, but in my heart, I know she knew there was more to life. I had many thoughts of what could have been, what she could have done, achieved, and experienced. Now, as I watch her fade away, in a manner that I could never have imagined, it makes me want to live my own dream to its fullest.

There was a conundrum for my mother. She so wanted me to be something, but she did not want to let me go. She felt that by letting me go and freeing me to become who I was meant to be would have left her behind. Despite feeling her pull, I did my best to have her walk beside me while I continued to move forward, both professionally and personally.

As I now watch her and speak with her in her state of dementia, at times sadness suffocates me. I sit with the sadness, knowing that at least I am physically with her and knowing also that God is with us. She knows me. We have wonderful conversations, and then sometimes she disappears in her mind.

I take countless photos that remind me of what I was feeling during the visit. I hold the memory that is being created before she will be gone. I let go of the negative feelings I have had in the past, and I use the sadness of her life as a driver for me to push through toward greatness. Deep down, I know this is what she wants for me.

Now, there has been a pause in my professional life as I deal with what is going on for her. We thought she was going to die, but she didn't. She is still very much with us. It has been an incredible time of being present with her, healing, and even documenting the special lessons of patience, compassion, and love during these most precious times.

Watching a parent die when it is not sudden is very much about letting go a bit at a time. Now, I feel at peace. I visit her. Sometimes she is not my mom; sometimes she is with me; and sometimes she speaks words that are not my mom's. But she is here. She is in wonderful hands; she is in God's hands.

And each day, I let go a little more. As I let go of Mom, I embrace me, Tanya the woman, and I show up as God wants me to. There is still much for me to do.

In late November 2020, Mom fell, broke her hip, and miraculously recovered. It was during this time and the months that followed that I felt the most incredible healing with both my parents, but particularly with my mom. It was during this time my eyes were opened, and I understood so much more.

On January 6, 2021, I wrote:

As difficult as this journey of my aging parents has been, there has been a hidden gift for me. It was this gift of having many questions answered, many "aha" moments, as well as opening my eyes that finally freed me. It freed me of this obligation I carried all my life to rescue them. To make their life better, to bring them inner, lasting joy.

Yet here I am at the end of their lives, learning more and seeing more, and had they not lived this long, I wouldn't have seen it. I wouldn't have learned it, and I wouldn't have seen it with my own eyes. This has been my gift. By being a committed daughter and taking care of them right to the bitter end, I saw so much of the truth. I learned so much of the answers to why things were the way they were, why my parents were the way they were, and finally, finally, I am free of the burden of trying to make them happy. Finally, I am free of a task that I have undertaken for nearly fifty years, an unachievable task. Finally, I can let them go. I have been able to let them go.

I am proud that I remained until the bitter end. I am proud that I have been able to hold myself and my marriage together. I am proud of me.

I am proud that I stuck it out and didn't free myself only when they died, because the truth is, I still would not have been free of the core chain. My parents would have been gone from this earth, but the cord would not have been broken. If anything, it could have been worse. If anything, I would have had regrets, what-ifs, and guilt that I didn't achieve the unachievable.

I am now free, they are free, and whilst they are still physically here, they are now in God's hands.

Chapter: 17

Acceptance and Hope Amidst Suffering

Even the most resilient of us never give up on the hope of a miracle. None of us want to accept reality and choose to stay in our blind faith, or denial, as some may call it. We remain there for as long as possible, since the alternative, reality, is not an option.

Acceptance still hurts too much. We dabble with it, we try it on, we put our feet in as if stepping into scalding water. We feel the burn, then we withdraw, knowing that the burn will bring lasting pain. We are not yet ready for that.

So, for now, we choose to not even enter the realm of acceptance and give up hope. That is okay.

My experience has been that there is a lesson (and good) in everything. We have a choice about how we look at the situation. We can focus on what is bad and only on what is bad, or we can search for a hidden diamond. It may be just a speck of a diamond, and we may not see it yet; however, we hold on to the belief that there is something beyond the pain.

My journeys have all had some form of good outcome. Despite tremendous pain, fear, and, at times, anger, good has arisen. Someone else, somewhere, has been helped by the stories I have told, the words I have written or spoken, and will be helped by the words I am now writing.

What a tragedy it would be to go through our painful life experiences and not reach out to assist others who need our help.

The people who want and need to know your story—how you coped—can be helped at their greatest point of need. You can provide them with not only a solution, but also hope.

When you are going through something for the first time, the notion of acceptance, faith, hope, and moving forward are unimaginable. It seems crazy to see anything good in what you are going through.

Those were my responses as well. I promise you, though, as I write this many years later, after experiencing hopelessness and despair, and a lack of willingness to move on with my own life, that this is no longer the case. A light flickered beyond the horizon that I could not yet see. All I needed to do was keep taking one step after another, and soon the light shone brighter. That light gave me the strength to keep moving forward.

Now, I love my life. I appreciate all my experiences, and I know without a doubt that I was guided by God, and I still am. Without those experiences I went through, I would not be the person I am today. I wouldn't have the resilience to keep going and have an impact on others who are going through similar experiences. There is a gift in everything, if we but allow ourselves to see it.

Chapter: 18

What Do You Say to Someone Who Is Dying?

I have sat beside several people during the end stages of their lives, and I know there will be many more. If you have not already lived this privilege, then I suspect that at some point in your life you will too.

In a recently published article that I wrote, I thought about what was the best way to help someone facing death. Let them go.

"Honey, you go now, it is alright. I will be alright." Those were the final words I said to my husband, Phil, before he closed his eyes and peacefully passed away.

To this day, I do not know where those words came from, they just naturally came. Little did I know that it was the most perfect sentence I could have said at that time. For Phil and for me.

So, what do you say to someone who is dying?

Grief is like a fingerprint, different for us all. It is one of life's unplanned journeys that we do not prepare for, nor are we given any instruction on how to navigate the rollercoaster of emotions we are forced to ride.

We feel guilt for even entertaining what we consider to be self-centred feelings. After all, how must it be for the person who is nearing the end of their life if we are going through so much ourselves?

Present grief ignites the flames of our buried, often unresolved, grief. Once we can identify and deal with our past stuff, then we will have the ability to put it in its proper place and be fully present with the one who needs us now. They are, after all, now participating in the most important act of their life, their final act.

So, this is why we step aside and make it all about them. We join them on their journey and allow them to take the lead. It may be that we calmly "be" with them as they ride their own rollercoaster of emotions. It may be that we are the quiet confidant, the secret keeper, that one safe haven they now have.

The journey begins well before those final breaths. It begins once one hears those horrid words—cancer, terminal, months to live, or "I am sorry to say..."

For many, often those first few days are their worst, and the rollercoaster is the most frightening. The shock, the fear of dying, the anger that you are dealt this hand, the lack of control of your body, your life, and the crippling uncertainty of what is beyond the horizon is almost too much to bear.

This is also the time when you show up for them, becoming a pillar of strength for them, even if you do not have the answers. You may not need to say a thing. You are simply a strong foundation for them when they need to fall into someone's arms. It is you who will be there to catch them, knowing that you have what it takes to hold them through the crisis. Remember, it is not about you.

Once the first tsunami passes over after the initial diagnosis, even if you do not know exactly what to say to them, walk beside them on their journey and be prepared for the next wave.

Expect the wave of anger to arise in them, because it will. Knowing this journey is often unplanned for many, you need to recognise they feel it is not how their life was supposed to end. You will hear, "I didn't deserve this," "It's not fair," and most certainly, "Not this soon."

Allow them to express their anger, sit with them, let it spew out, knowing that once they sit with the anger long enough, they will learn that its real name was grief.

Never forget that beneath your own confusion and despair are sadness and grief. You feel sadness for them, for yourself, and for everyone you have lost before them.

The end stage of life can also be alarmingly clinical and matter-of-fact. Become as informed as you can be about their situation: the diagnosis, the treatment, the consequences of the treatment, and anything else you feel the need to know. Such details can get in the way of precious moments when someone is at the end of their life. It can be very easy to be distracted with small talk or get in the way with your own curiosity. Silence and being present with someone are far more precious than filling in time with words that have no real meaning.

The days pass, and you want to make the days count. Therefore, place extra focus on your own self-care, or get the help you need to process your grief and manoeuvre through the emotions and the everydayness of your life. Neglecting your own care will not serve you or them.

This, of course, is as much your unplanned journey as it is for them. When you walk beside them gently and compassionately, the right words and actions will come easily and effortlessly for you. What a gift and a privilege for you to be able to walk beside someone during this most extraordinary time.

Whilst you may not feel it at the time, one day you just may be able to reflect on this journey with unspeakable gratitude that you were chosen to walk this path and experience love at its finest.

For many who have just been given a terminal diagnosis, regret knocks on their door, possibly not the first time in their life, however, this time the knock is more like the door being broken in.

They feel regret and sadness, not only for what they did not achieve in their life, but for not becoming who they knew they could be. Fear may have stopped them from attempting what they truly wanted in life.

Many, on the other hand, did not allow themselves to simply be their true authentic self, to own their existence, to own their worth.

Now just may be the time they decide to confront this. After all, what is there to lose? To now go within and find, feel, and be who they want to be, for as long as they can be. If you do not go within, then you take the risk of going without.

For those of you observing on the sidelines, this topic may be new, as you see a different side to your loved one or your spouse. It may be something that ever so slightly alarms you, or it may, in fact, be something you welcome.

Someone whom you have always known was there, however, now you are finally meeting them, experiencing them, even enjoying them.

Could it also be your time? For you to let go, show up, take down the barriers, remove the narrative of how you "should feel," and allow that fearful side of you to fade away. What a beautiful mutual gift one spouse can give to the other when they know their time is limited! If only we could do this without a terminal diagnosis also being part of the equation. We need to learn to show ourselves and experience true freedom; to embrace these moments of oneness and say what intuitively feels like the right thing to say. After all, in relationships, we have similar needs: to know that we are lovable, that we have been loved, and in the end, that our life mattered, as did we.

There does come a time to have the difficult conversations about the practical aspects of preparing for the end stage of someone's life.

What do you say when it comes to planning an end-of-life celebration? Who says it first, if at all?

This is often a conversation which, rightly or wrongly, doesn't happen. Neither spouse can say the word "funeral," or that "d" word, die. Many feel it is a conversation that will bring nothing but pain and a sense of the end looming.

Imagine how it could be for everyone if the meaning of these tough conversations is altered? What if, instead of the meaning being about endings, it was about joy, memories, celebrations, acceptance, and even new beginnings?

What if it was possible that even in the midst of what feels like challenging conversations and suffering, that joy, laughter, surrender, and acceptance were also present?

What if, throughout this entire journey, as you wonder what to say to someone who is dying, as you wonder how to process your own journey of grief, you were open to acceptance right at the beginning? Why wait?

What if, when you surrender to acceptance of what is, this allows you to show up with your loved one in a state you might have never known was possible?

When we don't make it about us, but make it about them, then there will be no concerns about what to say. You will be able to remain out of your head and stay in your heart as you listen and hear every word they say. You will feel what they say, and you will naturally know how to respond.

Meanwhile, you continue to walk beside them as they take the road never travelled before, until together you come to a fork in the road. This is when triumph begins, theirs in death, and yours in life.

Part III

• Physical Mastery •

Chapter: 19

Your Health Is Your Wealth

April 12, 2005, was to be the final day of Phil's life. I didn't know that he would take his final breaths later that night. We were told it would be two to three days, and he would probably be lost in a coma for most of it. Even though I physically remained by his side the whole time, a part of me would leave. I recall moving in and out of reality that afternoon. It was as if I left my body and hovered from above, watching a scene from an incredibly sad movie.

This is where the story of the ginger crunch comes in. During one of my episodes of emotionally departing the scene, I began to focus on the piece of ginger crunch I had the day before. I raced across the road from our home to buy some supplies, and bought this piece of ginger crunch slice for myself, and ate it at afternoon tea. I was so physically and emotionally exhausted, I just felt like I needed something sweet to replace all the adrenaline-driven energy that pumped through my then-tiny body.

Now here I was, twenty-four hours later, sitting beside Phil, holding his hand, obsessing about that exact same piece of ginger crunch. "How many calories did it have? Did I really need it? I won't eat so much today, as I probably ate too much yesterday." Then, bang, the thoughts would disappear, and once again I was present with Phil in the hospital room, and the pain of my reality would return.

This episode of the ginger crunch brought home to me how much my precious life was dominated by, and affected with, this crazy fixation with food, body image, self-worth, dieting, and everything else associated with it. It was a turning point. Here I was, obsessing over that bloody piece of ginger crunch and stealing what turned out to be Phil's final precious moments that day.

Even though I had already addressed my obsession with food for over two decades, it would re-emerge during stressful times. When the pain of my obsession became worse than the pain of addressing it, this journey with food turned out to be one of the most difficult to overcome. Over the years, I have discovered that a massive part of the population also is obsessed with food and uses it as a source of comfort, connection, or escape from life.

The tricky thing about having a food issue is that you just cannot stop eating. It is the fuel for our bodies, and we must face it every day, several times a day, and choose wisely in order to maintain good health.

Whether it be food, alcohol, shopping, online activities, gambling, drugs, whatever your choice of escape, the struggle is similar. It is not uncommon to give up one and swap it out for the other. For example, some alcoholics give up liquor only to obsess over food as a way of escape.

One of the greatest gifts of this massive journey with the food crazies was that, at a very early age, it introduced me to the importance of self-care. Not only my physical body, but also other areas of my health, such as my emotional well-being, my spiritual life, and even my intellectual health.

Whilst this journey may have started out being purely superficial because I thought I had to have a better body, as I matured, my desire to take care of myself stemmed from this deep desire to live a better, healthier life. I also realised it was not enough to just be motivated; it also took discipline and hard work every day. As they say, repetition is the master of all skills, and there is no way around it.

It can be very tempting to place so much focus on our material possessions—homes, cars, clothes—that we believe they are the most valuable. My mother would always say there was nothing more important than your health. My youthful response would always be "Yeah, yeah, yeah." I believed I was indestructible. It is not until some form of physical or emotional challenge knocks on our door that we pay attention and begin to invest in our wellness.

There is no greater equaliser with humanity than ill-health or death. This is when, no matter how much we have materially, we are all the same. Never in a gazillion years would I have thought that Phil would get cancer and die at the age of forty-eight. We lived such a healthy life. Nor that both of my parents would end up with dementia. Nor that one day, infertility would knock on my door.

Committing to and mastering our wellness is vital and requires our full attention and, in many cases, a financial investment. It also means believing that you are worthy enough to invest in your health and emotional happiness. This is often the block that stops people from doing something about their health until it is too late. The truth is, either way, the money will be spent. You either invest in your health and wellness early in your life, or you can spend that money later in life trying to regain your health back.

Therefore, I have dedicated an entire section to physical resilience, taking care of your most valuable asset, which is a healthy body. Throughout this section I will share with you some of my experiences, lessons, and strategies in the hope that it motivates and encourages you to commit to reaching optimal health, without waiting for an event to force you into it.

What changes, if any, would you like to see in your personal health? Why? What would be the consequences of not doing anything about it?

Chapter: 20

Food Freedom - A Common Story

This journey with a poor body image began when I was fourteen years of age and heading out to my first ever school disco with friends. This in itself was a big deal, as I was not allowed out much as a teenager, so I was super excited. It was the first time ever I wore a pair of blue jeans, together with a white, long-sleeved shirt, and a waistcoat. I felt as though I looked like the female version of John Travolta. For once, I didn't feel different from the other girls and felt part of the crowd.

I distinctly recall looking at myself from all angles in my bedroom mirror, feeling good about everything, then suddenly, I didn't. As I turned around and looked at my butt from a different angle, I heard this voice in my head tell me that it looked huge. It was in this precise moment that everything changed, and suddenly, I went from feeling pretty good about myself to feeling fat, unattractive, and different. Things were never quite the same after that night.

Being raised in a typical Croatian family, food was love. Every celebration was a feast. Preparation began days before the event, and there was never any expense spared when it came to food. We came home from school to a table laden with fresh baking, and no matter what emotion was present, we celebrated it with food.

I tell the rawness of this story simply because it is such a common one that many are too ashamed or embarrassed to share. My very unhealthy relationship with food affected every other area of my life.

This is also what I observe when clients come to me about their weight or food issues. It's not about the food; it is rarely about the food. However, because we never address the real problems that lie beneath, we keep thinking it is all about the food. If only we could get our eating under control and lose weight, everything would be fine. For many, including myself, this hideous cycle can go on for a very long time, and even reappear at various stages of our turbulent lives, as it did for me.

Many have said to me over the years that my eating wasn't that bad, and in hindsight, perhaps it wasn't. The accountant in me always kept track of the calories. Based on calories alone, no, the food wasn't that bad. My definition of a binge when I was a teenager was eating the normal calorie requirement of two thousand calories.

It is not surprising that I stopped menstruating for three years as a teenager. Looking at me, no one would have thought I was unwell. My lowest weight was one hundred and twenty-five pounds, and whilst it didn't remain that low for long, it was enough to jumble things up in both my body and mind.

Also, even at my highest weight of around one hundred and sixty pounds, I still looked normal, as I was so tall. Therefore, many never truly knew what was going on beneath the layers of this jovial extrovert who was known for being disruptive in class as a young teenager. It was the anguish inside me that was the killer—the emotional pain I put myself through, believing I was never good enough, that I was different, and flawed to the core.

My toxic thoughts kept me away from food, followed closely by the shame. Then, once again, I would begin the cycle all over again. Thankfully, I opened up to a counsellor, my doctor, and even found a twelve-step program, which was a wonderful foundation for my recovery during the past four decades.

This thing with food was simply the way I coped with all the other things in my life that I could not deal with. Sadly, my relationship with myself and food affected the decisions I made as a young woman, and thus affected the entire trajectory of my life. This was fuel for the cycle, and the more I used food, the more I felt shame and guilt for the bad decisions and for not being all together like everyone else. (Little did I know.)

This thing with food wasted a lot of my head space, which took away precious time from everything else in my life. At times, I was never truly present because I was either feeling full after a binge; feeling awful about myself; wondering what I should eat or not eat; whether to exercise; or whatever else I obsessed about at the time.

It affected the decisions I made in my life, and in my early twenties, I made some really bad ones. Relationship-wise, I didn't choose well. Whilst everyone else could see my professional capabilities, I didn't. Even though I made some bold decisions and they ultimately worked out well, I always wondered what would have been the outcome had I backed myself more. It took me a very long time to see my true talents, long after others had noticed them. I still didn't think I was smart enough to succeed, and it all stemmed from feeling so different from others. Plus, I had this thing going with food.

Then there was my physical health. Thankfully, I got off rather lightly, probably because my eating wasn't that extreme. I only thought it was. My friends would laugh at what I classified as a binge and probably felt rather proud of how much they could shovel in. Thankfully, I never could, nor could I purge, and for that I am unspeakably grateful. The sugar binges were not nice though, so if you are one of these people with a sweet tooth, the yucky feeling can last for some time and create some mighty headaches.

As an accountant, my allowable range of calories was not that low, and what I classified as a binge was not that high. It was rigidly controlled. Plus, I loved to exercise, and perhaps this was what kept me relatively healthy.

I knew the calorie content of most foods. I tried all the diets and all the weight-loss regimens. I even joined one popular organisation ten times (no kidding) in the hope that this time I would be able to stop binging. On one occasion, I put rocks in my jacket so that I was over the ten-pound threshold to be able to join. Most people would look at me with disdain, wondering what I was doing there in the first place.

I write about my poor self-image so extensively because it was such a massive hurdle to overcome, and one that many, many people suffer with. It is not uncommon for someone to present to me with a completely unrelated issue. However, once the food problem (or alcohol or other addictive behaviour) is sorted, then the remainder of their life slowly comes right.

Chapter: 21

The Solution Is Within

In the early days, there were many moments during my food journey that felt so bad, you would think it was enough for me to fix this problem once and for all, and not put myself through the pain.

I recall one Monday on university campus when all I wanted to do was throw up. In fact, I did. I knew it was a Monday because, yet again, I was eating ham and tomato for lunch that day. That's what I had been told to do. This diet plan was high in protein. Can you imagine a girl from Croatia surviving without bread? I cannot tell you how many times I commenced that same diet, eating that same Monday lunch. I doubt that I ever made it through the week to experience what the Friday lunch was.

Then there was the time in my thirties when I ate so much homemade, alcohol-laden cassata ice cream on Christmas Day that my sleep was more like a coma that night. I awoke the following day in agony from sleeping in an awkward position with my neck. It was immobile for days. I also had a sugar hangover that nearly closed my eyes. Despite this experience, my resolve to never eat sugar again lasted only three weeks.

By my mid- to late-twenties, my situation became intolerable, and this was what eventually drove me to want to fix my life. Slowly but surely, I began to address the issues within, and as a result, also conquered the food issues.

The more my eating normalised, the more I was able to go deeper into what was going on in other areas of my life, and make some big decisions. This was the emergence of Tanya the woman, not Tanya the insecure little girl who still tolerated the intolerable.

Even though I already knew the calorie content of most foods at this point, food was still just food. I didn't care about protein, carbohydrates, or what was good for this ailment or that ailment. In fact, I didn't know much at all. It was during my thirties when the stress of infertility and ill health knocked on my door, and I once again began to obsess about and sometimes use food to cope.

Firstly, I was trying every natural food combination under the sun to somehow increase my chances of getting pregnant. Coupled with that, during a holiday in the Pacific, I caught a nasty dose of staphylococcal, and ended up having the most wretched boils for eighteen months. It took an awful cocktail of drugs to drive the infection out of my body.

Hence, trying to detoxify after the nasty boils, and trying the natural fertility approach, totally screwed up my mind when it came to eating. I honestly wished I didn't know as much as I did about food and its effects on my body, as it drove me nuts. My obsession with food led to feelings of deprivation and binges that were brought about by trying to control my intake. In hindsight, I would have been better off had I just let it all go.

Over time, and after working diligently on my problems, things began to even out. Much of my healing took place in my late thirties. I delved deeply into what was really going on inside. I faced and felt the grief of not conceiving and built a muscle of resilience so that no matter what was going on in my life, I learned to not turn to food to soothe my pain.

At least until my forties. About six weeks after Phil's death, once people had gone back to their own lives, reality hit. The emptiness was real, and the pain of losing him was raw. This was uncharted territory for me. You can never prepare for the death of a loved one. I wanted to run from this new reality.

It was on a particularly dark, cold, and wet night in June 2005 when I felt so alone. My cat, Fergus, stayed close by my side. The grief was too much to bear. I didn't want to pray, I didn't want to feel the pain, I just wanted to escape, and the only way I knew how was to eat. My only saving grace was that, as I now lived on my own, I didn't stock as much food in my house as when I was feeding big Phil.

I went to bed that night in despair, torn apart by the grief. The extra food didn't solve my problem. Phil had died. I couldn't bring him back. Plus, now

I also had a belly full of peanut butter and jam, smothered with a topping of remorse. The darkness within me the following morning was so intense, I couldn't even open the fridge.

I ask each of my clients, "What is one thing you could change that would have a massive impact on every area of your life?" For many, the answer is to fix a food or substance problem. I then follow up with the question, "So why are you not doing it?"

It was a question I had asked myself many times, yet still, it never seemed bad enough for me to finally deal with this issue completely. I still clung to it a little bit. I managed my food issues, but never fully let them go.

The grief of Phil's death made me finally decide to wake up. I knew that this event had the possibility of tipping me over for life. The pain of staying in my food problem became worse than the pain of changing, so finally, I decided to stop wasting any more of my life.

His death became the pivotal point in my life. Up until then, I wasted my life waiting for someday—a baby, happiness—and as a result, I was not fully present today. I missed out on everything that I already had right in front of me.

So, I decided enough was enough, and I chose life. Not just existing, but doing my very best to live life fully and deeply. Making the decision was the first step. I didn't know how it would pan out, but I had to get honest with myself and finally be willing to let this food issue go.

The solution was within, and I knew that. I had to stop looking for answers outside of myself. It was time to finally get this monkey off my back.

Whilst I did not quite have the winning formula, I knew it would not be an overnight fix, but a recipe which also needed the important ingredients of patience, compassion, and kindness toward myself. I would do this, no matter what, for me.

Chapter: 22

When Giving Up Was My Answer

I clearly remember one day when something inside me just gave up. I was one hundred and fifty-five pounds at the time, and I let go of this need to be one hundred and forty-eight pounds. It was this difference of seven pounds that occupied my life, my day, my thoughts. It was seven pounds that had me starting something new on a Monday and binging by Thursday. It was seven pounds that kept me stuck in a cycle of craziness.

Thing is, though, it wasn't just the seven pounds. It was all the mush and pain underneath it, and this need to be exactly one hundred and forty-eight pounds. The obsession with those seven pounds was what stopped me from delving deeper into the roots of my behaviour.

So, my solution was to give up, throw in the towel, and make peace with those seven pounds. One day, I gave it all up, all the rules and restrictions around food, dieting, counting calories, and labelling food as good or bad. I learned to eat when I was hungry and feed my body what it wanted.

I gave myself permission to eat whatever I wanted, even if, once upon a time, I labelled it as bad. I gave up restricting myself and allowed things to not be perfect when it came to food. As a result, the desire to binge on those restricted foods slowly left. If I found myself starting to pick or slightly overeat, I said it was okay to just stop and not annihilate myself for the remainder of the day. I gave up endlessly punishing myself by expecting my eating, my life, or me to be perfect.

This strategy worked very well for me; I simply made the decision to not overeat. No matter how bad I felt, or what was happening in my life, I would not binge on excess food. Did it mean my eating was perfect? Definitely not. Did it mean that I had a balanced, nutritious diet? No, but I didn't care.

Anything was better than binging.

On many an occasion, I would start to overeat, and the only way I believed I could stop was to throw the remains in the garbage or down the kitchen disposal unit.

These were some of the extremes I went to during those early days to get through a day without binging. If one day all I had for dinner was toast and not one scrap of vegetable or protein, then, so long as I wasn't binging on excess food, I was happy with that.

My only outcome was to stop needing and using food to run from life. I did not put myself on any eating regimens or exercise plans. I decided to trust myself, listen to my body, and learn to be present while eating, and, most importantly, while living.

Acceptance was the answer to so many of my issues. Prior to my decision, I had to control, resist, or run from discomfort. However, when I learned to accept life on life's terms, then the need to control my food and body also left me.

This was a process, and it did not happen overnight. It took me a very long time to no longer be tempted by the next new diet that promised fast, lasting results. I got to the point where even thinking about starting something like that would throw me off. Always, every single time, the thought of deprivation, rules, and rigidity had my face in the refrigerator for yet another last supper before the Monday start date.

It took me a long time to trust myself. Yes, all the books out there were probably great, but there was never a book written specifically for me, and the only person who could ever author such a book was me. So, I decided to listen and trust myself and learn the difference between physical hunger and emotional hunger.

Let me also add that my identity when it came to my physical body was one of strength. I no longer wanted to be skinny. I wanted to be strong and feel strong. This helped me change my relationship with food. It became fuel for my body, enabling me to function at my optimal level, both physically and emotionally.

I also developed a strong certainty within myself that no matter what food was placed in front of me, even if it was the most amazing smorgasbord, I could choose to eat whatever I wanted and know when to stop eating.

So long as I remembered this, then, even through the most stressful episodes of my life, I remembered what had worked for me in the past and remembered my strong identity. Yes, sometimes I slipped, but I had the recipe to get back into line again. It was a conscious decision.

These strategies are what I continue to use today, and at the age of fifty-seven, I am fit, strong, and in very good health. However, most importantly, I am free from my obsession.

If you have identified with anything I have written about this topic, and you want to change, then I invite you to also make the decision to free yourself. Whether it be food, alcohol, or any other substance or behaviour that is stopping you from becoming your best self, let me remind you that everything is possible. It is never too late, nor are you ever too old.

Chapter: 23

The Importance of Knowing Your Why

There is a quote by Jean Baer, which says, "The change of one simple behaviour can affect other behaviours and thus change many things."

When I was training to be a Tony Robbins coach, the one phrase that I heard repeatedly was, "How you do one thing is how you do everything." This line was the perfect summary of what I knew to be true about my issue with food. Unless I changed my eating habits, then every other area of my life would continue to be affected.

This is precisely why I ask my clients the same thing. What is that one area of your life that, if you changed, would then go on to make a radical change in every other area? We still repeat the same old unhealthy patterns because our *why* is not compelling enough. It is not until we hit absolute rock bottom that we finally decide that *now* is a good time to stop.

Unfortunately, shame often stops us from owning our problem, taking responsibility for it, and sharing our issue with another human being. The thing about food is that you feel so embarrassed not to be able to moderate one of the most basic of bodily needs. After all, a baby could do it. A five-year-old can do it. And yet here I am, in my adult life, not knowing when to stop eating, drinking, or doing whatever else it is.

There were many reasons for my decision to finally fix this problem, and my reasons were big. In fact, they were so big that nothing would have taken me back to the craziness and emotional self-torture I used to put myself through.

Firstly, I didn't want to hurt myself anymore. I came to a healthy place of self-respect and self-acceptance. I healed that little girl inside who never felt good enough. That little girl had felt enough pain, and now it was time for her to dance, as little girls should.

Tanya, the woman, emerged, and this woman didn't need food for love, for comfort, or for certainty. Tanya, the woman, met her needs in healthier ways. I now liked who I was. I decided, once and for all, that I would never harm myself with food ever again. I felt deserving of joy. I felt worthy.

There was also the pain and the gift of watching someone fight for their final breaths. Here I was, with life handed to me on a silver platter and drinking from a golden goblet, instead of declining what life had so generously handed me.

It seemed that, in each decade of my life, my *why* became stronger, partly because I was always on a path of personal development. I have this deep desire to continue to become the best I can be and to experience as much as I possibly can of this beautiful life.

Another big *why* for finally addressing my issue was that, if I didn't, I would not be able to fulfill my purpose. I believed there was a greater vision for me, a purpose for mankind, and it was my responsibility to show up and deliver. Whether it be for a family member, my clients, my work colleagues, the readers of my books, or the listeners on the radio, unless I was fully present and clear-headed, speaking openly and honestly, then I did not feel I was authentically serving mankind.

This is why I was happy to open up about my eating issues. By doing so, I would free others to speak up and, as a result, begin their own healing journey. To be open, transparent, and serve others helps me to remain committed to my own journey of physical wellness.

I wonder if you might resonate with some of what I have written about. It doesn't need to be a food issue that you have; it may be another substance, addiction, or perhaps behaviour that gets in the way of living your true purpose.

Might you be able to carry out your legacy now, your contribution to the world? Are you ready? If not, what is one change that needs to happen in your life for you to be able to carry out your purpose during your lifetime? Why is now the right time? What will your life look like if you don't do it now?

So many big questions, right? I invite you to find your *why* and decide.

Chapter: 24

Self-Care – Investing in Your Greatest Asset

There were a handful of lines that my mother would repeat to me time and time again. However, the one she would say the most was, "Tanya, you have to look after yourself and your health, because no one else will do it for you. You have to do it for you."

She understood the theory of it, however she struggled to put her own words of wisdom into practice. No matter how hard she tried, she always put the needs of everyone else before herself. As the years came and went, she would then add, "It's too late for me, but not for you." She was angry at no one but herself for not doing more to meet some of her own needs.

Now, at the age of eighty-nine, as she lay in a rest home, her concern is still for everyone else and that we be okay should something happen to her.

This is such a common story, for both men and women, who give so much to others in their lives, yet find it so hard to receive, to accept, to allow themselves to be taken care of, nurtured by others, or even do the same for themselves.

Seeing this exact trait in my mother has given me the gift of contrast. To see her physically work without ceasing, pushing herself to a point of exhaustion, was something I observed in her. Whilst I did pick up on some of those traits myself, I made the decision to not follow in her footsteps. I learned the art of self-care very early in life.

Journaling was how it began, and has been a regular practice in my life to this day. If I was to name one of the most valuable tools in my personal development and emotional care for myself, I would say journaling was in the top three, and one I regularly share with my clients.

In my early teens, my need to be thinner overtook my life, so I admit my journey of physical self-care was purely superficial. I wanted to be slim and look good on the outside. End of story.

The way I did this was by walking, although it wasn't fashionable to walk back then. In fact, many people laughed at me as I walked for hours at a time on our neighbouring streets. When my dad joined me, they laughed louder at this father and daughter who they saw walking for miles.

At seventeen, when I commenced university, I followed in the footsteps of my brother Nick and began lifting weights. It also wasn't fashionable for a young woman to do such a thing back then, however I liked the idea of becoming stronger. A part of me liked to do things that were different and out of my comfort zone.

I never missed a day of journaling, and soon, I fell in love with the notion of personal development. I became an avid reader of everything I could get my hands on regarding the improvement of self. I began to invest in countless books on the subject, and this has continued to this day.

Commencing self-care at such an early age has without question benefited every area of my life. I felt the benefits of motivation and discipline when I didn't even know I was searching for it.

I just knew that writing in my journal every day kept me still, close to God, and close to me. I also knew that whenever I went for a long walk, I felt better. When I lifted weights, I felt stronger. When I swam, I felt a sense of freedom. When I read something inspiring, it made me want to be better. When I practiced any form of self-care, I felt better, so it made sense to practice it every day.

Whilst the internal narrative to be slim lingered inside during much of my late teens, the journaling and exercise taught me the benefits of repetition and discipline. Consistency worked. My daily rituals and habits soon became a part of me. They were part of my identity.

Whilst, during particularly stressful times in my life, my approach was unbalanced and I would overexercise, I was aware of what I was doing and trusted that I would find my happy medium again. Over time, I discovered what worked for me, and that sometimes, less was more, and quality over quantity was the healthier approach.

I worked out my winning formula for optimal health and self-care, which became so ingrained in me that discipline also eventually became part of my identity and helped me to achieve in many other areas of my life.

Unlike my mother, from a very early age I did nice things for myself. My big brother Zel took me to a fancy salon for my first haircut, and he took me to have my ears pierced. I loved the hairdresser, the beauty therapist, having a massage, and other similar treats. I was fortunate to have a job as a teenager, so I had the money to continue treating myself.

It also taught me that when I couldn't afford those luxuries, then I had to find other ways to do these nice things for myself, even if it was painting my own nails, or walking along the ocean. All these things made me feel good and taught me the importance of not waiting for others to meet some of my needs. It is important that we allow ourselves the gift of optimal health, and self-care is one of the important ingredients.

There are so many ways you can take care of yourself physically, emotionally, spiritually, and intellectually. The trick is to find out what brings you joy, what makes you happy, and then write them all down. Create your own treasure chest or toolbox of self-care activities. Make it a large collection with loads of variety you can choose from, and then decide when you will allocate the time to do it.

Every week, pick at least one from your list, make a date with yourself, and just do it. It is as simple as that.

Chapter: 25

Selfish – No Way!

Some may say that self-care is fluffy, a waste of time and money, and is self-indulgent. Yes, some forms of self-care cost money, and some cost a lot. By the time you add up the wholesome eating, gym memberships, life coaches, therapists, whatever it is that you invest in, it certainly adds up.

However, there is so much you can do without it costing a fortune. In some cases, the only cost is time. Yet still, we find excuses not to treat ourselves. As I have heard it said, if you cannot find ten minutes in your day, then you haven't got a life. This is why I ask the question, "What will it cost you if you don't do it?"

What costs even more is when you get sick, or do not change some of those habits, which keep you poor physically, financially, emotionally, and professionally. The lost income, treatment costs, the cost of overeating, drinking, a broken marriage, are just a few of the financial costs of not taking care of yourself.

Some may say that I am a little extreme when it comes to my decisions on self-care, and my response is, I had to be. The alternative just wasn't an option for me. I have left jobs, broken off relationships, moved my house, and said no to people because I knew that in some cases, they were harmful to me.

I have been known to cancel social engagements simply because I needed solitude. People have not understood, and I just had to let it be, as it was enough that I understood. I began to trust my instinct and what I needed, especially during times of intense stress, so I put my well-being first. I wasn't saying no to others, or rejecting them, but finally I was saying yes to me because I needed to.

Does self-care mean that I am going to live a longer life? I don't know. Anything can happen. However, what it does mean is that in the time I have left on this earth, I am going to be in the healthiest and most energised state possible. My actions are about being fully present with life. Taking care of myself is one way to do that.

Self-care is not selfish, it is necessary. A leader or a parent cannot lead, parent, or love another from an empty vessel. If you feel self-care is selfish, then simply let it go, as you may run the risk of being stuck in guilt every time you do something for yourself or riddled with resentment for abstaining.

Let go of the rules, let go of the need to be liked, of being the consummate giver. Let go of being mean to yourself. The alternative is that either way, you may become stuck. After all this time, I am rather black and white when it comes to my personal well-being. It is non-negotiable in my life. How on earth can I serve my clients, my readers, and my audience if I don't take care of myself? How inauthentic would that be?

I'm curious. What needs to happen before you will allow yourself to say yes to your well-being?

Chapter: 26

Movement – Just Get Up and Do It

I will never forget the day I attended a hospital appointment with my eighty-something-year-old father just after he had his fourth major cancer surgery. When asked to remove his shirt, I gasped. He looked as though he had just been chewed up by a shark. Yet to my father, the only thing he wanted to know was how soon he could go fishing again.

My mother never stopped. At eighty-nine, the only thing that halted her forward movement was a nasty fall that broke her hip and bones in her back. Many people her age would not have survived. Despite preparing us for her death, she is still very much with us and doesn't plan on going away anytime soon.

Which is why, four weeks after Phil's death, I put my exercise gear on, went to the gym, and started lifting weights again. It was why, only a few weeks after that, I jumped back in the pool and felt the freedom of the water flowing over my body. It was why, as each year passes, I commit to staying physically strong, exercising, and taking care of my one precious body.

The truth is, you just need to get up and do it. One of the reasons I have such huge respect for my parents is because that is exactly what they did. The word "can't" was not part of their vocabulary. They took no sick days when cows were waiting to be milked at 4:00 a.m., when four children under the age of nine needed to be cared for. They just got up and did it. That is resilience.

One of the greatest lessons I have learned about exercise is that if you don't enjoy it, chances are you will not keep it up. Over time, I discovered what I loved to do and have continued it all these years.

It was no longer about needing to be thin or burning off calories; it was about feeling like Tanya the Amazon woman, the woman who was energised, strong, and committed to her health. It was also about understanding that moving your body is the fastest way to change how you feel, so, every time I did exercise that I loved, I immediately felt better and wanted to do it again soon.

There is no need to teach you about exercise, as you can find anything you need online about what you can do, how to do it, and how to commence. The one thing I will repeat is that, no matter what you decide to do as your form of physical exercise, make sure you enjoy it, and you feel great doing it.

I always like to ask my clients to remember a time when they felt physically strong, fit, and in optimal health, so, I will ask you the same. Do you remember a time when you felt great about how you looked, your exercise routine, and it showed in how you moved and lived your life? Knowing that you have done it before, been there before, what is stopping you from doing it now? If you have felt like a strong Amazonian woman once before, or a fit, strong, masculine man, then, of course, you can do it again.

As the saying goes, movement is medicine, both physically and emotionally. Decide to move your body again, come up with a compelling reason why now is your time, revisit what you love doing, make a plan, find a mentor if you need to, and make a start. I cannot say it any more simply than that.

Chapter: 27

Step It Up When Things Are Down

Eating too much, not eating, having binges that go on for days, drinking that extra glass or two at the end of the day, having weekend drinking benders, taking uppers to stay awake, and downers to get to sleep. You name it, when adversity knocks on our door, taking care of ourselves is often the first thing to go out the door.

Under normal life conditions, we need to treat our bodies as we do our most valuable assets, because they are. They need to be regularly fueled, nurtured, and treated with the utmost respect to exist in the demands of today's environment. Once we add to this the pressures of running a home or business, or holding a demanding position, then we need to pay even more attention to it, ensure all our tanks are full, and have a greater awareness of what is going on in our lives. Our health is our wealth, and without it, we are broke.

As we age, and especially during times of intense personal trauma or life transition, then we need to take care of our bodies even more. While the effects of the stress may not show on the outside, we don't know what is happening to our bodies on deep physical and emotional levels.

We exist on adrenaline, very little sleep, and lots of caffeine, or whatever substance we use that keeps us going. We don't feel good and see only the tip of the iceberg, until suddenly, we are forced to stop when the physical and emotional effects begin to manifest.

Hair loss, weight loss, weight gain, extreme fatigue, skin irritations, insomnia, racing heart, boils, painful periods, and mood swings are but a few of the signals I have experienced in the past to make me eventually stop and take note. When we do not listen to those initial signals, our bodies will start screaming in other ways.

In hindsight, during my most traumatic life experiences, I am astounded as to how I could physically function and achieve as much as I did on such little sleep and poor nutrition. I was surviving, but not much more, and I was not aware, nor emotionally able, to focus on my physical or emotional well-being.

Eventually, the crash will come, of that I can assure you. When you do not listen to your body, it will break down. If this is you right now, then take note. Reach out to someone for help.

These are the times when you need someone close to you to help you through. It is not a time to be stoic and brave, or tell others you are okay, if deep down you know you are not.

This is why I emphasize self-care so much. Even if you are not going through tough times, self-care is about keeping yourself adequately fuelled, with plenty in reserve, when life dishes out the unexpected. And sooner or later, it will.

Chapter: 28

Don't Let a Bad Day Turn Into a Bad Week

Despite developing a healthy, respectful relationship with your body, self-care is not an overnight fix. The decision to change once and for all can be made in an instant, however, it can take some time to create healthier habits and see real, long-term results. For those who are impatient, though, even a week is too long to wait!

Progress is progress, no matter how small or how slow. A kickstart with a quick result can be a good thing to initiate some momentum, but know that the end result is what you are after. Your success will take tenacity and grit. Once you are truly committed to your outcome, then even if you have a bad day or take a step back, the trick is to never give up on that final goal.

The power of an obsession can, at times, be rather frightening. You think that everything is humming along nicely, then suddenly you find yourself having a not-so-good day. So, you might turn to food, alcohol, drugs, or overexercising to soothe yourself.

Even after one piece of chocolate, no change on the scales, or a day when you miss exercising, it is very easy to fall into the trap of believing that you have blown it all and may as well go on a self-destructive bender. Whatever the slip, is you believe there is no way out and start on the downward spiral of ruining the rest of the day or week. Don't be so hard on yourself. You are human! How easy it is to pull up a chair at the refrigerator, open another bottle of wine, or perhaps go online and spend money you can't afford to spend!

This is where a force within you needs to rise and say, "No! I will not do this to myself." You need to remember why you started your journey and what you want to achieve. Remember all the time and energy you have invested in your journey.

When you believe in yourself and that your health is your most valuable asset, then you can stop the downward spiral. After all, this slip isn't who you are anymore; this is no longer part of your identity. You now have the strong identity of an empowered, disciplined human being who puts their well-being first at all costs.

This is when you stop, remove yourself from temptation, forget about what has happened, show yourself some compassion, remind yourself of how far you have come, and start fresh. Do not place pressure on yourself to rectify your slip. It happened, and you are human. Today is not blown. You only need to change your attitude.

Take really good care of yourself and take a curious look at what triggered your behaviour. Learn from it, call a friend, and discover the tools to prevent it from happening again. Keep learning from your little setbacks, but don't let them destroy you.

When you have time, journal about your feelings to discover what drove you to spiral downward. Feel your emotions, write about them, and look at them straight on rather than pushing them away. Running from a problem or a feeling only creates another problem for you.

Finding your personal winning formula is a process, and, over time, you will continue to build various strategies to help you during these crucial times when life throws you off. Always stay curious about why you feel and act the way you do. Instead of feeling so serious about your slip, try being playful. Instead of berating yourself and expecting perfection, let it go, even laugh about it, knowing that tomorrow is a new day. You have learned a new lesson.

For example, do you need to break the pattern of falling in a heap on the sofa after work? Is that what leads you to food or the bottle? If so, find an alternative behaviour. Try exercising at the end of the day, take a shower as soon as you get home, or call a friend. Do whatever it takes to break the pattern.

It takes willingness, determination, persistence, and strength to move forward when you have slipped. Remember why you started on this journey in the first place. Remember what it feels like when you take care of yourself, when you feel emotionally and physically strong. Remember how good it feels when you show up professionally, when you are present in your relationships, when you are clean.

These are all strong reasons why your path to self-care and wellness is vital. The result must be so compelling and feel so good that nothing will get in the way of achieving it, feeling it, and living it. Nothing.

Remember, it is not about how many times you fall, it is about how many times you get back up again. Dance with the setbacks, laugh with them, laugh at yourself, and never give up on yourself.

Chapter: 29

Make Optimal Health a Place You Want to Go

Whilst pain and hitting rock bottom were my biggest drivers to stop doing something, what drives me now is my desire to feel pleasure. Instead of having the bloated belly from too much food or the foggy head from too much sugar, I'd rather feel energised, alert, happy, present, and unstoppable.

Being stuck in our old, painful patterns is not going to give us what we ultimately want in life. Making the decision to change, and sticking to it, will.

The truth is, I like being in shape. I like wearing nice clothes that fit me well. I like showing the world I am happy and not a victim of my circumstances. I like to be an example to others. I like to feel as though I am contributing to the world, instead of hiding away within the walls of my home. But to be able to do all those things, I need to take care of myself. I say once again, your health is your wealth, so invest in it.

Create such a strong reason why your goal is so vital that nothing will stand in your way. The way to ensure you remain committed and consistent is by making this part of your life a place you want to go and spend time, guilt-free! In fact, make the importance of your well-being your top priority.

If you are a business owner, treat yourself as your most valued client, until you believe and know that you are your most valued client. If you are a parent, as they say on the aircraft, put on your own oxygen mask first, then you can better serve and protect your family.

Eliminate "should" from your language and create a more exciting and energising way to describe your wellness routine. Always remember, you are on this journey because you love how it makes you feel. This is now who you are.

If you feel self-care sounds too fluffy, then find another word to describe it, and do your best to get beyond the airy-fairy feeling you have about self-care. If I was to define what self-care means to me, I would use words such as energised, happy, joyous, strong, relaxed, playful, and creative.

When this sacred place of self-care becomes a must in your life, then you will notice the excuses disappear. You take responsibility for your wellness and your happiness. You will fully understand the importance of finally saying yes to your health, and it will be a place you want to be every single day, simply because it feels so good!

Part IV

• Loving Again Later in Life •

Chapter: 30

Recap Your Relationship with Self

One of the worst nights not long after Phil died was when I burned a pot of chickpeas. I left them boiling on the stove after an emergency sent me racing out of the house in the early evening. Three hours later, I returned to discover the fire alarm screeching and my home filled with thick smoke. The chickpeas were a hard lump at the bottom of a very black pot. All four levels of my home had a cloud of smoke so thick I could barely see.

All I could do that night was open every single window and door on all levels to allow this suffocating smoke to exit. Unfortunately, it was one of the coldest nights of the year, so I had to put on as many layers as I could and then curl up in bed with Fergus.

As the smoke slowly left my home, my eyes were stinging less, and I could breathe better. However, what replaced the suffocating feeling I had from the smoke was the suffocating grief that replaced it. I slept little as I lay there freezing in bed with Fergus.

It was moments like these that reminded me of the reality of the bigger picture. Phil died, I am now on my own, and I must do this thing called life on my own.

The stress from this event created such an enormous tsunami of grief that it is only in hindsight that I can now look back and understand why, during those early years, I made some of the choices I did.

Never would I have thought that loss and uncertainty could be so powerful when it came to the decision-making process. Despite all the work I had done on myself for all those years, deep down I was still vulnerable and hurting, and there were many more lessons for me to learn in life, especially when it came to other people.

As I reflect on that time now, I see things clearly. When clients come to me in the state I was in back then, I know what they are feeling. However, when you are in the depths of grief yourself and have lost that personal foundation of self, sometimes you cannot see a thing.

Over the course of my life, and especially during the past sixteen years, I have made some not-so-good decisions. However, I have also made some fantastic decisions. The way I learned how to make good decisions was to master everything I had written about in the first half of this book. Mastering my emotional and physical state and building an unshakeable sense of self and resilience has been key to fully trusting my own decision-making process, especially in terms of what I will and will not tolerate in life.

Did it mean I always made good decisions? No. But I continued to move forward to fix my bad ones. It was by making good decisions that I built the muscle of having the confidence to not remain stuck. These are the same tools I offer to anyone who comes to me asking how to navigate life.

What I do know is that every decision made impulsively from a place of fear or loneliness has not served me well, nor do I believe it will serve you. Whilst it is difficult to be patient when you are hurting, I encourage you to learn how to not be attracted to quick-fix solutions. The alternative approach is to feel what is going on, be patient as you go, listen, and then take action.

We all have a desire to love and be loved in our lifetime, and there is no question that loving again later in life is different. Well, it was for me, and it didn't come without a few lessons.

Throughout this section on relationships, I am going to share with you some of those lessons of mine while on this journey of love.

My intention is to give you enough examples to think about what you could do differently in your life when it comes to love. It is my hope to save you some time from being overwhelmed, experiencing heartache, and wasting money, as you learn to walk this road called life, and make great choices on how, and with whom, you now want to share it.

Chapter: 31

Overcoming Loneliness

I will get straight to the point; loneliness is painful. It has always been a major problem and has driven people to make poor decisions, perhaps too quickly, especially when it comes to love.

With the state of the world and the isolation that many must live with, loneliness is in itself a pandemic of pain.

Loneliness, or the fear of being alone in the future, is also a reason why so many people keep repeating the same mistakes. They remain in unhealthy relationships, feeling stuck and unfulfilled, or they choose badly to start with, because anything is better than being alone.

If reading this makes you feel a bit uncomfortable, please keep reading. I invite you to be brave and face this issue head-on. Trust me, it will be worth it.

If only we would stop running. Running from boredom, running from ourselves, running from the present moment, running from life. If only we would stop running from feeling lonely or the overwhelming fear about the future, and instead, remain still for long enough to just feel our emotions and be present with them. Feelings will eventually pass.

Without question, I have done my fair share of running in life, but I didn't experience running from loneliness, or being alone, until after I was widowed.

What I mostly struggled with was *what I felt* when I was alone, full-blown grief. It was not that I wanted someone near me or with me, it was that I wanted to run away from the paralysing grief I felt when I was alone.

It was during these times of being alone in the stillness that the tsunami of grief would wash over me. That is what I ran from, the reality of the darkness that Phil had died, and he was never coming home. Facing this reality was my greatest pain, and, at times, simply too big to deal with.

It is why I always explore with my clients and ask the question, what lies beneath the loneliness? A big question, I know, and not one to be answered immediately, however, a question I invite you also to ask yourself. Take a close look at the truth of why being alone is so painful.

Interestingly, what I also discovered was that being alone not only brought out my grief, but it also brought out my happy memories, which then turned back into grief again. As an example, you are watching a great movie on your own, or you receive good news, and you want to share it with that special someone in your life, then you remember that they are no longer there.

There are so many ways loneliness triggers this need to run from the present moment. For many, they are driven by the desire to find a new partner before they are ready. Sadly, low self-worth, lack of personal boundaries, and uncertainty about who you might meet one day, or not meet, are also drivers to connect in a romantic relationship before you are ready.

Sadly, when you decide to be in another relationship before you learn how to be in a relationship with yourself, you miss out on what is best for you.

Eventually, I decided that it was wiser for me to be alone and feel the loneliness and grief. I realised that I was making decisions from a place of uncertainty and listening to everyone else's opinions instead of paying attention to my own gut feelings and instinct.

If you believe that a relationship is the way to fill up this big empty void within you, the truth is loneliness is possible even when you are in a relationship. Don't believe that what everyone posts on social media is the true picture of a relationship.

Many believe they are not lovable enough, not rich enough, or too old, so they settle. They tolerate behaviours in relationships that are well below their line of non-negotiables when it comes to respect. Have you ever felt unheard, disrespected, or made to feel as though you were unlovable? Have you ever waited for the phone call, the card, the slightest term of endearment as some evidence that you were not the only one making all the effort in the relationship?

Many of us have, and this type of inner loneliness was far worse than the loneliness of being single. At least, whilst on your own, you have 100 percent freedom and control over what you will do with your life. You hold the remote, so simply get up and change things!

You probably want to know how a person overcomes loneliness. How do you reject the temptation to date before you are ready?

What has worked for me personally, no matter what the circumstances, is to master my emotions. Make friends with that feeling called loneliness. No matter what feelings come up for you, acknowledge them, embrace them, feel them, learn from them, and then let them go. It is as simple, and as difficult, as that.

Sometimes feelings are not nice, however, the feeling itself will not kill you. Take one day at a time, one breath at a time, and do whatever it takes to get comfortable with discomfort. The only other alternative is to keep running away and doing what, up until now, has not worked.

Whether it be your faith, friends, hobbies, exercise, more study, or other forms of self-care, decide to do whatever it takes to learn and love how to be with you.

The notion of feeling *complete* when you are in a relationship doesn't sit well with me. I invite you to be complete in your life, so that when a relationship does come along, it will enrich your life.

Meanwhile, take this time to learn how to nurture yourself, learn how to be playful and have fun, do all the things you have given up on in the past, and find out what brings you happiness. Instead of waiting for someone else to take you out on a date, why not take yourself out on a date? Where would you go?

Now is the time to get excited about your life, so I invite you to make a list of all the things you can and want to do, and dive in today, this week. Why wait?

Chapter: 32

Be You First, Then Part of a Couple

When you are already in a committed relationship, it is quite easy to express your observations of those around you in the dating scene. "Oh, why would he bother? She causes him so much grief," or "Why on earth would she settle for someone with all that baggage when her life is so much better on her own?" We have all done it.

My point is, never judge someone else's journey because we never know what is happening in their lives. The truth is, they know the person they are with is not even worthy of their time, but still, they are driven by loneliness, grief, or low self-esteem.

This also creates an underlying pressure and judgment for those who are not in a relationship yet and want to be. The societal pressures may be subtle, but so is the pressure we put on ourselves to be part of something, which is why many settle for someone who is not good for them, or they remain in an unhealthy relationship. After all, many believe it's better than appearing to still be single, or so they think.

Isn't it so much nicer walking into a dinner party with a partner or having someone to take to a wedding you have been invited to? Isn't it lovely to even be invited? I have heard many stories from those who are newly single that the invitations from their married friends slowly dry up.

If you find yourself in this place, then speak out and let your friends know you would still like to be included in the group. You may need to take the initiative to say, "Hey, I am coming over for a visit, is that okay with you?"

How often have you, as a woman, been asked, "So, is there a man in your life at the moment?" Also, alternatively for a man, "So, haven't you found the right one yet?" One of my girlfriends got to the point of responding, "No, because there are so few out there!"

Then, if you have been dating quite a few people recently, you are asked, "So, who are you dating now?" The truth is, sometimes you must kiss a few frogs before you find your prince or princess. Instead of staying with the wrong person, the right move is to move on.

The world of dating is now vastly different from what it once was. In some ways, it is not as safe with the online world, so if you feel you are being judged by your peers, do your best to let it go. It can be hard enough dating in today's world without adding a layer of shame on top.

The presence of social media, and even some advertising, can create a sense of urgency and hammer at your self-worth. It can be tempting to fall into the belief that the reason you are not in a relationship is because you don't look like the person in the advertisement, or your life is not as exciting as everyone else's on social media. This can also place added pressure on you to do crazy things to your own body because you don't believe you are physically attractive enough to be worthy of love.

All the above can make you rush into a relationship, to feel that unless you are part of a couple, you are not as good as the others. What I invite you to do is, before diving into a relationship with someone else, focus on building a healthy relationship with yourself.

If you are in a relationship now and something feels off, then it probably isn't right for you. It can be tempting to believe you can *love* the red flags out of someone. It won't work. Learn to listen to your intuition because it's likely it is trying to tell you something. Just be you and learn to like you first before you enter a relationship that hopefully will be much healthier.

It takes courage and deep honesty to look in the mirror and be prepared to take responsibility for your life. It means a willingness to take ownership of your past decisions and a lot of compassion toward self so that you do not beat yourself up for years to come. It takes humility to make amends when we have wronged others, and it takes bravery and tenacity to pick yourself up and be willing to try again.

This journey is a personal one, and one of the things I didn't do well was trust myself. I felt pressured by other people in my social sphere. Be vigorously honest and take the time to do what you need to do to be able to say, "I am okay with me, before I want to be part of 'we.'" Close your eyes and ears to any pressure, internal or external, that says that to feel whole, you need to be part of a couple.

Only you know when the time is right to love again. Go within and fall in love with yourself first, so that when you start to date again, you take your true, authentic self on the date. There is no need for pretense, a mask, or a liquid diet before you meet someone. Say to yourself, "This is me, and I love me!"

When you meet the other person, ask the same of them, that they just be themselves, even on the first date! Their true self will eventually emerge; it always does.

Chapter: 33

When Is the Right Time to Love Again?

There is no right or wrong answer about when is the right time to fall in love again.

When you have taken that journey within and are able to know who you are in the world, where you are headed, what you want in your life, and why, then you will have the confidence to explore an answer about your next intimate relationship.

By that time, hopefully, you will have worked on areas of your identity—trusting yourself, setting boundaries, and being able to say no to what doesn't feel good in your life.

I have heard many examples where the right person entered someone's life, leading to a successful relationship. It might be eight years from now or only three months after being widowed.

Many feel they are not good enough to be in another relationship right now. They feel broken and unlovable, and are still waiting to ensure that all the boxes are ticked before they allow their next love to show up.

So, when will you know? What will be your indicators? As the saying goes, waiting for someday is another form of avoidance and can lead you down a path called nowhere.

Remember not to feel as though you, or everything in your world, needs to be perfect in order to be ready. None of us are perfect. Just keep living, enhancing yourself and your life, and then embrace whatever life brings your way.

Know you will have baggage, and so will your new partner. You can heal together. There will be much healing and grieving to do even when you are with someone new.

Be ready to help each other unpack each other's baggage. Don't look for someone to save you; look for someone to stand beside you as you save yourself.

There is no doubt about it. I was still grieving on some level even after Grant and I were married nearly five years after Phil's death. Despite the healing that still had to happen for me, what I did know for sure was that he was the one whom I wanted to share the rest of my life with. Was the timing perfect? Who knows? Thankfully, we both had enough compassion and respect for the other to allow our own stuff to emerge and heal.

Prior to meeting Grant, I was still in full-blown grief and had no idea what I was doing. Deep inside, I was still haunted by grief, whilst on the outside one would never have known.

There was still so much pain buried within me—the craziness of my twenties, the grief of not having my own children, feeling so totally lost as to what I was going to do with my life, and then Phil's death. It took me a long time to see and acknowledge that there is only so much a human can take before they fall apart.

It took me a long time to forgive myself for falling apart and not doing things perfectly when I should have known better. It took me an awfully long time to not allow shame into my life for not coping better.

If this is you, if you relate to any of this, then I invite you to take the time to heal and forgive yourself. I was lucky and found a kind, loving, compassionate, caring man with whom I was safe to do this.

When you are kinder to yourself and show yourself the compassion you deserve, then you will have a far greater respect for yourself and will have a deeper knowing of when you are ready to love again.

The thing is, you will not have to go out there looking for the one, nor will you want to, as you will be too busy living and having fun, doing what you love, and meeting your own needs.

When you are ready and open, you never quite know who or how someone will appear in your life. Sometimes, letting go and going with the flow of life, even when it comes to love, is the best way to go.

Chapter: 34

How Do I Know What I Want in My Next Relationship?

The best thing about making mistakes is that you get first-hand experience of a tough lesson, and you never forget it. The best thing you can do with that lesson is learn from it and not repeat the same pattern.

Also, you get to help others by not making the same mistakes, either by leading by example or mentoring them to not do the same.

You learn the art of forgiveness, forgiveness of others, and mainly of yourself. You learn the importance of letting it go, forgiving yourself, letting go of the shame of making mistakes, and moving forward with your head held up high.

The other wonderful thing about dating people who are not right for you is you begin to learn what you don't want in your next relationship. If you find yourself repeating the same pattern, then that is your big signal to pay more attention to what is really going on for you. What needs does this type of person meet for you? Learn and address it for the last time!

What has enabled me to go on to help so many other women and men in my work was a direct result of my bad choices and experiences. My past experiences enabled me to smell a rat very quickly and say, "No thanks."

My past experiences, the difficult ones, are what have helped me to become as resilient as I am today. Without those poor decisions, I would never have learned the art of being able to make good decisions.

Not-so-good choices are what eventually help you to make the right choices when it comes to love. My gift from those difficult choices was the great ones I eventually made later in life.

What my experiences taught me was to step back and address what was really going on for me. What was really going on? Oh, that's right, grief was staring at me again. I had to face my grief again and take a deep, honest look at why I had not moved past that part of my life.

This meant rejecting victimhood and blaming everyone else for my mistakes. I had to own them all and take responsibility for my life, my choices, and where I was headed from now on. It meant asking myself some big questions and being vigorously honest with my answers.

Questions like, why do I want or need to be in a relationship? What needs am I trying to meet, or am I still running from something? Is it that my life is empty, and I believe that a relationship will complete it, or am I now ready to truly share my life, my joy, and myself with another person?

Is it that I need someone else to fill the emptiness inside me, or do I want to enrich my life, as well as someone else's life? How would I like my life to be enriched, spiritually, emotionally, intellectually, and physically? Can I do this myself, or am I expecting a new relationship to fix me?

The questions could go on; however, it does mean staying still and possibly single for long enough to face your questions and answer them with absolute honesty.

Another good strategy is to know what you *don't* want and what has not worked well for you in the past. Reflect on those patterns you keep repeating, the ones that hurt, yet you still fall for the same type. Write them down, write everything down that you can think of that you no longer want to feel, that you no longer want to experience, that you will no longer tolerate ever again.

The next thing is to write down everything you do want to experience in a relationship. What do you want to feel in your next relationship? What are some of the characteristics that you can love in another person? What are some of the characteristics in yourself that you would love to share with another? What are some of the adventures you want to experience with another person one day?

Many people come to a bottom line of what they will and will not tolerate anymore. I was no longer ready to compromise my own values and beliefs for the sake of a relationship. I was no longer willing to tolerate unacceptable behaviours or habits. I was not going to enter a relationship unless it in some way enriched my already rich life, and unless I had something to give. What was the point?

I invite you to do the same, as this will open your eyes to what is really going on and stop you from running from your truth. Your goal is to arrive at a happy place with your life, so much so that you want to share it with someone else.

One last thing... When you are ready, you will know. A big part of this journey of greatness is to trust your instinct; when it comes to love, that will be the biggest takeaway I share with you. Trust your inner voice and your instinct. Trust you.

Chapter: 35

Learn to Listen to the Hunch Inside

Whenever I would see a particular phone number come up on my iPhone, I would think to myself, "Oh, that's that nice man, Grant, from the Honda dealership. I think I will take that call, as he is such a nice guy." And he was.

Grant and I met about eighteen months before we began dating. My initial gut feeling, and what I discovered about him over time, was that he was kind, a gentleman, and incredibly professional when we had business dealings. He was rather quiet; however, I saw a depth and simplicity to him that was endearing. My hunch about him was spot on.

The greatest gift I have learned over these past four decades was that I finally learned how to follow my own instinct and not listen to the noise around me, especially when it came to love. It can be easy to be thrown off by the opinions of others around you, some well-meaning, some not, who claim to know what's best for you.

When it came to dating Grant, I was nervous and, in some way, I didn't trust myself because of some poor decisions I had already made. Whenever I would feel unsettled, mainly because others would thrust their opinions on me, I would take myself away to a quiet place of peace and reflect on what I knew to be true.

This was where I would find my peace, still my thoughts, and remember that I knew more about me than anyone else. I trusted my instinct more than I trusted the words of others.

Finally, I had learned not to ask others what they thought, because every time I did, my decisions were not good. When I reflect on some of those not-so-good decisions, the first time I laid eyes on a particular person, my reaction was off-putting. I didn't listen to my instinct back then because I was still running from the pain, and I wouldn't admit it.

Whilst working with clients who are in an unhealthy relationship, I ask them the same question: "What was your initial gut feeling when you met them?" I have yet to hear a positive response. In fact, many are quite vocal about what they felt when they first laid eyes on their prospective date.

Yet, something drives us not to follow our instinct, to ignore that uncomfortable feeling inside. Instead, we move forward, forgetting that initial response, and then look outside of ourselves for reassurance or certainty that we are doing the right thing. We also ask our friends, many of whom are not in a good space themselves, what they think.

When the relationship begins to sour, you then reach out to those same friends, once again asking them what you should do, instead of asking the person who already knows and is experiencing it firsthand, you.

When it comes to love, take that precious journey within, learn to trust yourself, and that initial feeling you have the first time you meet someone. Continue to listen to yourself throughout the relationship. If something feels off, then listen to that hunch inside, as it is probably right. If something feels right, you will know it before anyone else does.

Chapter: 36

Loving Again After Loss

Grief is a funny old thing. Just when you think things are feeling easier, a new tsunami of pain rolls in and takes you out. Not always as intensely, or perhaps for as long, but those waves of pain still come. This is what I wrote in my journal after a year of being in my new relationship with Grant.

August 1st, Sunday morning, in front of the fire. I am feeling very well, and I am really noticing how my emotions, even though up and down, are so much more stable recently. This winter I have given myself the permission to process and feel and revisit my grief. Even though I feel comfortable, am settled, and in love with Grant, the grief still appears. It is only this year that I feel as though I have been able to fully process, let go of some of the deep pain, and allow myself to move forward with my life again.

As we settled into the normality of a relationship and the knowledge that we would spend the rest of our lives together, it was as if my entire previous five years were coming back, and the reality of what I had just been through. I have had to return to feel my loss, my pain, and simply stay in the present moment. Sit with the grief, do my best to be present with my life now, and acknowledge that this was how everything would be from now on.

Yes, Phil had died. (I hated to use the D word.) My other two cats were also gone; my home and garden were all gone. My dream of having my own children was gone forever. Here I am now, in 2010, starting a new life with a new life partner, yet still I weep.

Poor Grant had been tested and tested, as I was so aware of my own lack of boundaries and vulnerability. I had placed huge barriers up for myself and raised my line on what I would and would not tolerate. It took me such a long time to trust myself again.

When we first started dating, I trusted no one, not even me. I observed Grant as if he were a chemistry experiment. I watched how he interacted with my family, my friends, and, most importantly, with my cat Fergus (who, at this stage, knew best). It was important to treat Grant as Grant, not as someone who might be something a bit like Phil, or needing him to be like Phil, or comparing him to Phil.

This time, it meant letting go of my previous life, which I still held on to, and at times, very tightly. I had to let go of the dreams and plans that Phil and I created, and be present with the dreams Grant and I were building together. Grief still somehow connected me to my past life, and I understood that letting go of the belief that I still needed to be grieving was a big part of allowing myself to now move forward, be happy, and let others see I was happy.

During this time, I would ask myself some strange questions to ensure I was truly following my heart. One was to imagine if the entire world was to fall around me, there was nothing left, it was the end of time, who would I want to be standing next to? In a heartbeat, my answer to this crazy question was always Grant.

Loving again later in life is different. Loving again after losing someone to death is different. There were so many layers I found myself exploring and moving through. It was about loving Grant for who he was, not the parts of Grant that reminded me of Phil, not the parts of Grant that filled the gap in my life. It was about knowing and being present with the reality that this was permanent, and we were combining our lives, past and present, and creating a new future.

The reality for me was that it took many years to allow myself to fully embrace being in a new long-term relationship. Thankfully, Grant was patient. We have been together twelve years and married ten. As each year progresses, I allow myself more and more to embrace life again, let go, feel free, and fully embrace joy again.

But guilt would sneak in time and time again. Guilt for moving on, guilt for being in love, guilt for flourishing as Tanya, a confident woman in life, being true to herself, and chasing her dreams. The inner belief for so much of my life, and one I was always working toward changing, was to stay small, and not show up to fully embrace who I was now. Once I entered my forties, and then even more so in my fifties, I finally cracked open my shell and stepped into the world.

This was one of my greatest obstacles to overcome when Grant and I got together. Allowing myself to be happy, and, most importantly, allowing the world to see that I was happy, without wondering what everyone would think.

For me, loving again after loss meant putting aside being vulnerable and bringing my true self to the relationship. I was determined to not hold myself back ever again, not in love or in life. Thankfully, once again, I have been blessed with someone who is happy to walk beside me as we both explore this road together.

Chapter: 37

Keep Being You

One of the greatest frustrations I hear when it comes to being in a relationship is the struggle to keep being yourself. Over time, things change; you change, someone else changes, and before you know it, you become lost in the relationship.

Perhaps you find yourself becoming like the other person, being available for them at all times to meet their needs, whilst putting your own needs on the back burner. Over time, you forget who you are, what you need, and completely forget the person you were before you came into the relationship.

I won't deny that I, too, have done this. I had the perfect teacher, my mother, who always put the needs of everyone else before her own. She served the entire family on every level before she took care of her own needs.

What lesson did I learn observing this behaviour from my mother when it comes to relationships? It is that I must allow myself to take care of myself, to remember that a relationship is about meeting each other's needs, and to always continue being true to myself.

The way to do this is to become comfortable with the discomfort of saying no to others. Every time you say yes to someone else and put their needs above your own, you are saying no to yourself.

If this continues, then over time, resentment builds, the suffocation becomes unbearable, and because there is nowhere for this frustration and anger to go (because you don't want to be seen as being angry and resentful), this rage implodes. It manifests in numerous ways. We overeat, we drink, we self-harm, we spend, we do anything to not let others see the level of anger that lies beneath.

If you cannot openly share your feelings or be your true self from the very beginning of a relationship because you fear you will not be enough, or loved by this person, then it may be that this is not your person.

If over time, you lose yourself in the relationship, then take note and ask yourself why. You cannot build a relationship using sand as a foundation, as this will not be enough for it to hold strong when the heavy rain of life comes, and it will.

Sometimes the solution is to simply communicate how you feel to your partner. They may not even be aware of what's going on for you. It will be fresh territory for them as well.

Also, as I so often say, most of our answers lie within. Start asking yourself some honest questions again. What am I not doing? What am I tolerating? What do I need to say? To whom? What needs to happen for me to have the courage to voice what is going on inside? What needs to happen for me to just be me? The questions could go on.

Everything you need to know is already there, and it may be that you need to flick a switch and make the decision to just be you again.

Chapter: 38

Maintaining the Love

The way my father courted my mother was like nothing you would ever hear about in current times. He lived on an Island called Korcula in the Adriatic, which was part of the former Yugoslavia, now known as Croatia. My mother lived along the coast in a small village alongside the Neretva River called Opuzen.

What stretched between my father's home and my mother was the Adriatic Sea, plus a river. He was so in love with my mother, he would row his boat across the twenty-mile stretch of ocean, then somehow get to her village from there, to take her dancing.

That is not all. At times, this small boat would also have a forty-gallon drum of diesel on board, plus his rather voluptuous sister, Lilly. This was what my dad used to do just to see my mom in those early days. I have often reminded him of this when he would moan about doing basic chores for her later in their married life.

They were so in love. He was her first boyfriend, and after being together for nearly three years, they married at twenty years of age. I cannot tell you how many times my mother has told me that she loved him, for better or worse, simple as that, which is why they have lasted nearly seventy years together.

My opinion on what it takes to have a lasting relationship later in life, and not one loaded with drama, is the importance of choosing correctly right from the start. Yes, doing this may take a little more time, however, it will be worth it in the end.

To help you choose well, perhaps go back and read everything I have already written. This book contains the lessons I learned to help me finally choose well. You want your next relationship to be one based on who you are today, what your current beliefs and values are, rather than one on who you used to be, or where you are still trying to recreate your past.

Whilst I know that maintaining a relationship requires work, a part of me doesn't like to use that word. When you are both prepared, when you understand your own needs and the needs of your partner, when you have a deep mutual respect, then hopefully it won't feel like work.

It will require a regular maintenance plan of open and honest communication, patience, compassion, respect, playfulness, a mutual path, and a deep desire to be committed to each other and said path, no matter what life throws your way.

Does it mean the journey will always flow beautifully? Probably not. However, when you are with the right person, you have a desire to help each other be the best person they can be. If one is struggling, then you help them unpack their stuff, just as they help you unpack yours.

If one is grumpy and possibly hurts you emotionally, always believe that their intention was not to hurt you, it was not deliberate, they just mucked up.

If you muck up, apologise without delay, and let go of the drama. If you find you like to hang on to the drama and have some back-up ammunition for later use, then you are the one with the problem, not them. Learn to let it go.

When you forgive, you forgive. It is a decision. You do not forgive with conditions and hold on to drama in reserve to fire back at them. If you do, it means you haven't forgiven them. Work together to unpack and sort out whatever is going on so that you can swiftly move past it.

If you begin to doubt yourself, or the relationship, or find you are constantly being critical toward your partner, then I invite you to remember what attracted you to them in the first place. What did you love about them? What was it about them that gave you 100 percent certainty that helped you decide, without question, they were the one?

Do not let doubt or anger fester. Let go and remember all those things that caused you to love them. Write them down if you must!

Another strategy to maintain the love is to continue to build on your dreams together. Create vision boards together, write down your deepest desires together. Do it regularly, make it playful, do whatever it takes to keep the excitement present and your dreams alive.

If you have a deep spiritual life, or one that's even mediocre, then pray or meditate, and do it together. Make prayer a must in your daily lives. Believe that no matter what problem comes your way as a couple, you can, and will always, move through it together.

If there is a consistent problem with addiction in the relationship, bring it out into the open as soon as possible and get help. Whether it be food, alcohol, drugs, spending, whatever, address the issue immediately, as the cost of not doing so is too great. It is difficult to have a third party, such as alcohol or any other substance abuse, in the relationship. There is no room for genuine intimacy with that other party lingering.

Take responsibility for your own stuff. If you tend to blame, compare, or criticise, then take ownership of your behaviour and learn new ways of dealing with your own stuff. Remember who you are with now. Continuously comparing them to your past relationships is one way to escape the current one. How easy it is to run from the present moment, even when it is beautiful!

The secret to the success of my relationship with Grant, after being together for twelve years now and feeling more fulfilled each year, is a mixture of all the above, and probably more.

Remember, part of the key to having and maintaining a beautiful relationship is to feel whole and fulfilled with yourself. Just be you. As the saying goes, when you get yourself together, then everything else will come together too.

Part V

• My Search for Purpose •

Chapter: 39

What I Instinctively Knew

Everything happened so quickly after the funeral. Within days, I instinctively knew to find a new home and move out of the one Phil and I had shared. I found the perfect place within forty-eight hours of starting to look, bought it the first day I saw it, and had a settlement date of about three weeks later.

All I needed to think of next was to pack up our existing home, sell the goods I couldn't take with me, and then move. Once in my new home, all I wanted to do was set up the basics I needed to sleep and eat, and the rest could remain in boxes.

I didn't care how long it took, nor that my new home wasn't fully furnished. I just knew to keep following my instinct for the days ahead, and everything progressed smoothly. Apart from that, I had no idea what I was going to do with the rest of my life.

There were two significant events that screwed up my plans and completely threw me off my axis: not having children and then Phil's death. The part of me that had craved certainty and control over my destiny was also brassed off, to say the least.

I spent my thirties waiting around for a baby, then much of my forties I went back to basics and worked out who I was and how to find meaning and purpose again. It meant really going back to basics, taking one step at a time, one day at a time, and, in some cases, one breath at a time. It was the only way.

When I focused on the fear and uncertainty of my future, then that was what I felt. When I fell to my knees, surrendered, prayed, and trusted that God had a plan for me, even though I didn't know it, then I felt an element of peace.

Soon after I had moved, there were two significant moments that occurred for me. The first was the absolute certainty that I needed to write the book and tell the story that Phil so wanted to write. I also knew it was important to share my story as well, for the twelve months after his passing.

Phil never had a title. He simply spoke about writing a book one day. Once I began seriously writing, the title *Unplanned Journey: A Triumph in Life and Death* was born.

The other thing I had certainty about was that, one day, my passion was to work with people at the end stage of their lives. They did not have to be at a place of acceptance of their fate. In fact, some might be like Phil. They had a diagnosis and were not prepared to give up hope. It didn't matter.

What I knew without a doubt was how much I had already helped many people who had been given a diagnosis. Walking beside many, including Phil, as they prepared for their final act, was the most rewarding work I had ever done in my life.

I had no idea how either of these would come into fruition, but what I did know during that dark winter of 2005 was that, once I moved into my new home and began to have glimpses of hope for my own future, these ideas were naturally born.

Chapter: 40

Everything Began with a Dream

All I ever dreamed about from the time I was about four years of age was to be a wife and mother. I had a collection of teddy bears and dolls, all of whom were my pretend children until my real ones came along. I couldn't wait to be a mom!

By the time I was seven and had decided I wanted to be a hairdresser as well, my collection had grown, and they had now also become my customers. Poor Mrs. Beasley was my most regular customer, and so, she had the least amount of hair left. Mr. Big Ted, thankfully, had very little to trim, so he got off lightly.

Having sported a Farrah Fawcett hairdo in my teens, the idea of wanting to be a hairdresser for others had worn off as the maintenance involved in doing my own hair was enough.

While I didn't really know what being a professional businesswoman meant, this was the dream I began to have. You might say that I created a fantasy in my mind that one day I would be something. Even though I still desperately wanted children, I also wanted to be a businesswoman, and I created this identity in my mind that one day this would be me.

I didn't even know what that looked like, yet I just knew that one day I would carry a briefcase. In fact, during a counselling session, I recall drawing two images of me. One as a very sad, stuck young woman, more like a little girl, and another as a confident woman in a business suit carrying her suitcase.

During the session, I distinctly remember looking at both pictures, feeling what it would be like to be in the shoes of both. When looking at the first picture, I felt trapped, and at the other, I felt free. That day, a part of me chose the latter.

Growing up, I had never really put any thought into what I would major in at school. What I did know was that my parents expected me to go to university. Since I excelled at mathematics and accounting, working toward a Bachelor of Commerce was the natural choice.

From an early age, I continued to long for freedom. Combined with a need for variety, both led me to have a colourful professional career. I made some bold decisions and brave pivots in my career, and, despite the surprise and pushback by some people, there must have been a determined and gutsy side of me because I did it anyway. When I was no longer fulfilled after achieving said goal, I would not feel that something was aligned, so I moved on.

Chapter: 41

Dreaming Without Work Doesn't Work

There are a few memories I will never forget while growing up, and one of those was the day I came home from school with my report card. I was in what was then the fourth form, so I would have been around fourteen years of age. The report wasn't good. Not only were the grades poor, but I was also apparently disruptive in class and an all-round nuisance.

Mom was in the kitchen, and I was hiding in the lounge. Once she had read the report, she stormed toward me waving it in the air and proceeded to give me a verbal thrashing that I probably deserved. I knew I could have done better. She didn't show Dad; she knew better, plus, she didn't need to. To me, Mom was scarier.

When I reflect on that day in the lounge, I feel so unspeakably grateful for Mom telling me off. It turned out to be one of those pivotal days when I made a decision that impacted the remainder of my life.

What Mom didn't fully comprehend was the depth of my self-doubt as a young teenager. This doubt was so ingrained in me that, at the beginning of every school year, I would dread the first day back. A darkness would fall over me, and it would hang around for a month or so until I settled into the new year.

I truly thought I was dumb, that I was different, that my parents had strong accents. My command of the English language wasn't that great, and I believed we were all different. I had been laughed at quite a lot at school already, and, as a youngster, was mocked in front of the entire class when I didn't know the answer to a math question. So that led me to also believe I must be dumb at both English and mathematics.

Mom's verbal thrashing when I was fourteen changed everything. I made the decision to stop acting out and see what happened when I worked hard. It truly was as simple as that. I decided to study harder, I decided to not mix with some of the people who I knew were not good for me, but most importantly, I decided to try and not give up on myself.

As a result, the following year, my School Certificate year, I did very well indeed. The year after that, my sixth-form year, I was at the top of my class in many subjects, including mathematics, and was fourth in the entire sixth form in mathematics. I excelled in accounting, economics, and even did well in English.

The biggest change in me, however, came from within. Instead of always feeling like the dumb girl who was different from everyone else, my identity changed. I had a taste of what it felt like to feel smart, poised, and confident. More importantly, I experienced what it felt like knowing that I did it. No one else got those high grades for me, and the way I did it was by doing the work and changing my focus.

I focused on doing well, on achieving, and once I had a taste of it, I kept going. Once I became top in some of the exams, I knew I had it in me to be top of the class. I knew I had it in me to come home with a report card to feel proud of.

This change in my identity from feeling like a dumb outsider to an intelligent, hard-working, tall girl who now felt proud of her height was a game changer. Knowing I could change how I felt about myself in an instant was what helped me in many areas of my life, particularly when it came to tenacity. My strong identity was like my mom and dad's, a hard worker who never gave up.

I created so many dreams for myself after Phil passed away, and I still do. At times, I think, "Dang, this is going to be such hard work." However, when I know for sure it is what I want, then I keep dreaming, I keep going, and I keep believing.

Many times, I have no idea how it is going to get done, so I stop being stuck in the how and focus on what my heart desires, what I believe is my purpose. When I reflect on some of the things I have achieved, it was my belief, mixed with tenacity and acting, that always got me there.

There have been many obstacles, pivots, and changes in direction in my life. What I would always do is continue following my instinct and working hard toward my goal, trusting that everything would eventually unfold as it should.

Journaling has been an amazing motivator for me professionally. I keep a separate belief journal, where, over the years, I have documented all the times I was bold, courageous, or made brave decisions. I have also documented all God's miracle moments, those times in my life when I could never have orchestrated such a perfect outcome in my life, and yet, it happened.

I continue to write in my journal every day. Mine is a beautiful, big, colourful book and is such an amazing resource to remind myself of what I know to be true. That belief in self, plus faith, and a lot of hard work, make our dreams come true.

A belief book, or journal, is also a wonderful reminder to yourself of who you are during those moments of self-doubt and uncertainty. In an instant, you can pick up the book and read about everything you have accomplished, how hard you have worked, and what is possible in life, even if you have no idea how it will all unfold.

If you haven't already created this journal, I invite you to do the same as I have. That way, you have documented actual evidence of events that have already happened in your life. Whenever you doubt your courage and boldness, or what is possible in your life, then go back and reread the list in your journal to remind yourself. I still do.

Chapter: 42

Make Room for Boldness in Your Purpose

Growing up, I always looked older than I was. At eleven, whilst being a bridesmaid at a wedding, I was asked out on my first date. Wearing a long dress with my hair up in petals, I looked closer to twenty.

As a seamstress, my mom would create the most beautiful clothing for me. Whilst I didn't like the attention from boys, I really liked looking nice in my lovely dresses and fake fur coats, which were so fashionable back in the 1970s and 1980s.

The good thing about looking older was that when it came to stepping out of my comfort zone, a part of me pretended to be older, bolder, and braver. The number didn't matter to me or get in the way. I had blind faith and did some things that kids wouldn't normally do.

After my first job at age fourteen in the department store, by the age of sixteen, I was a sales representative with my own company car! Not long after that, I had saved enough money to purchase my own car for five thousand dollars, which was a lot of money back then.

On a personal level, at around the same age, I took myself off to a therapist to find out why I felt so different from the other girls, why I felt dumb, and why I often felt so sad. I wanted to feel better, and without telling anyone else, I looked for help.

My bold decisions continued. The reason I had a fabulous job at sixteen was because I decided to take my final year off from attending college. Instead of studying, I felt confident that I could make it all up during my first year at university, so I decided to take a gap year. I applied for a big job and got it. It was as simple as that; then I commenced university the following year.

After completing my commerce degree, I became an auditor and accountant. Realising very soon that this did not stimulate me at all, I decided to become a flight attendant with our national airline. Yes, you read correctly, and many were shocked at my decision. Even the airline said they nearly didn't employ me as they had never had an accountant decide to become a flight attendant. I had my reasons, and I also had a plan.

My plan was to transfer to another position within the organisation after a few years. So, after nearly three years of flying around the world, I was offered a role at the head office.

My biggest desire, though, was to work for myself one day, to be self-employed. I didn't know what exactly, or how I would do it, but I just knew I wanted to be my own boss.

After a few years in the corporate airline world, I walked away from a good job to the role of self-employment, with no clients, just a dream of being my own boss. I was only twenty-seven. Boldness opens doors of opportunity.

Without boldness, after Phil passed away, I could have easily curled up in a ball and not found my true purpose or clarity on the direction of life. Not only did I have to fill the gap of not being a mother, I also now had to fill the gap of not being a wife, and at forty, the chances of motherhood would be slim. I had to do something, and I wanted it to be big.

There was no choice but for me to move forward and make that move sooner rather than later. I had to be bold. I had to take some chances and risks. What I chose to do was to believe that if I kept following my heart and taking action, then eventually my life would unfold as it should.

Despite being raised with an overcautious mama who tilted more toward fear than adventure, over time, I had to make decisions that she wasn't happy with. As much as I loved my mama, Tanya, the woman who had more of her father's crazy boldness, had to take over.

Ultimately, no matter how we are raised, this is no longer an excuse. No matter what age you are now, put on your big-girl or big-boy pants and follow your joy, follow your bliss, follow your heart, and ultimately, you will know you are going in the right direction.

By my late teens and twenties, I had education and career on my horizon. I made the decision to pull my finger out and work hard and realised that I was capable of being more than I thought. In my twenties, I did not really understand anything about my life's purpose; it was all about work and going through massive change.

It was in my thirties that I was introduced to the notion of purpose. It stumbled on me really. It was not as if I decided to suddenly find purpose in my life. Rather, it evolved. Very early in that decade, I became a go-to person for help. People who needed guidance, prayer, or support came to me. Then came the influx of people around me who were diagnosed and suffering with cancer. It seemed rampant.

At this point, my work was great, and I always had plenty of it. But being an accountant and IT specialist no longer made my heart sing. Simply having the reward of the material world was no longer enough, and whilst I still wanted to be paid, I also needed to feed my soul.

The most important things I had discovered were through the pain surrounding me; being there and of service to others was what I loved to do and gave me purpose in life. During my mid-thirties, I commenced my diploma in counselling, and interestingly, grief was my favourite topic.

My life was feeling very complete at this point. I was now forty and still with no baby; however, I felt okay. I felt happy and, on some level, accepting of my life, despite not having my child... yet. I was nearly at the end of my diploma and felt that the decision to do this was perfect. The counselling and mentoring fit very well with my commerce, so I was able to help my business clients professionally, and now also personally. I felt I had purpose.

Then came the shock diagnosis to take out all my plans. Within days of hearing Phil's news, I had a deep knowing that everything else which had happened in my life during the ten years prior was all an apprenticeship for this big event. Only now was my true purpose beginning to be revealed.

Chapter: 43

Follow Your Joy to Find Your Why

To find your joy, you must love what you do. During my search for meaning, especially during my forties, the best thing I did was to revisit my personal values, remember what used to make me happy, and notice what now brought me joy by just doing it. This took time. However, the more I began living my truth and learning how to just be me, the pieces began to come together.

No matter what family or friends are doing, what they think you should be doing, or what everyone on social media is doing, I cannot stress how important it is to take that journey within. To get your mojo back, to know what brings you satisfaction professionally, and to discover all of this, even if you are still grieving. Whilst you may not see what is beyond the horizon for you professionally, I encourage you to take the first step.

I am the first to admit that I spent a lot of time and money zigzagging here and there, trying various things, chasing what looked like the easiest route to fulfillment or what might have been the "in" thing to do at the time. In hindsight, I wish I had followed my own instinct right from the beginning, as ultimately, I knew right from the start.

There was also another hurdle to get over for me, and for many whom I speak with, and that is the notion of *allowing*. Of allowing yourself to move forward again, to live again, to achieve, and even be successful again. Allow yourself to rise and let the world see you are thriving again. Instead, we play small and do not unleash that part of us inside that knows we can be more and contribute more to the world.

This is a stumbling block for many, even if they have not been through a major loss. Many do not follow their hearts or what they are truly passionate about in their personal or professional life. What still gets in the way are those stories of not being good enough to succeed, or what would people say if I failed?

Regaining your confidence again, learning to trust yourself when it comes to your decisions, will enable you to take that leap of faith and follow your passion. When you have certainty and clarity in one area of your life, other areas will be affected as well.

You will know and feel what your true purpose is, the big reason you have for being here. You will develop a natural desire to self-actualise, to be the best you can be, and then turn it around and share your message with others, along with the legacy you will one day leave behind.

If you are searching for meaning and purpose in your life right now, I invite you to ask yourself some big questions to obtain clarity on what and why. Ask yourself questions like: What is the legacy you want to leave and why? Why is this purpose important to you? Why do you want to feel these experiences in your life? How do you want to contribute to the world? What is your message to the world and why do you want to share it?

Your why is what will keep you going. Your why is what will keep you grounded and at peace.

Whenever I got stuck, I would always come back and ask myself these same questions: What do I really love doing, what brings me joy, when I am at the end of my life, how would I like to be remembered? What do I believe God wants of me? How can I be of service to mankind? How can I turn this event around in my life so that somehow mankind can benefit from what I do from now on?

When I feel my answers give me peace, then I know I am on the right track. I invite you to also find your joy, find what brings you peace, bliss, happiness, and believe that what is possible for others, is also possible for you.

Chapter: 44

Letting Go and Moving with the Flow of Life

My decision to study toward a diploma in counselling in my mid-thirties was partly driven by my own grief in not yet conceiving. I figured that if I was going to have to wait to be a mom, or worse still, not be one, I had to do something more meaningful than simply being a computer consultant. I enjoyed it, but there was a depth to me that was not being fulfilled.

Also, I knew I was grieving all the time. I had a deep fear, a knowing inside, that I would never have my own baby. I am not sure where that feeling came from; it was just there. I accepted it. However, I did not let it stop me. My studies most definitely helped me on this grief journey, and I was also able to help others on their own grief journeys.

Despite knowing I was in full-blown grief, within months of Phil passing, I made the decision to get off my butt and start, well, something. All I knew was to just move and work toward doing something meaningful with my life and to teach others how to as well. Things fell into place, and before I knew it, I was studying to be a life coach and then a business coach. Life simply flowed forward.

The other thing I knew to do was to dream big dreams and plan even more. I created large, audacious, colourful vision boards, documenting all my personal and professional dreams. I bought large artist-block sketch pads and filled each page with timelines, graphs, lists of desires, and lots more. I put all of it on paper so I could see it. The more colourful and out there it was, the better!

The task of working alone was worth it, as the more I wrote, dreamed, and documented my goals, the better I felt. I cut out pictures of holiday destinations I wanted to visit, concerts I wanted to attend, spas I wanted to treat myself to, and even the colour nail polish I would paint on my nails. The process made me feel great, abundant, and excited about life again.

I cut out images of the books I wanted to write, the speaking engagements I desired, and the pilgrimages I wanted to walk on. These images and desires filled my soul and brought sparkles of joy amidst the grief that forever hovered as well.

In short, I just kept believing, praying, and trusting that if I at least dreamed, then I had taken my first step. I never forgot that moment in the kitchen just after Phil passed away when I had a deep knowing that there was a far greater plan for me in this lifetime, and that one day, I would know it.

Whilst I didn't know how it would unfold, I just trusted and had faith in the flow of life. I kept putting one foot in front of the other, kept taking action, even if I made some bad choices, but at least I kept walking forward. When I made a wrong decision, I made another to try and correct it.

Thankfully, during my counselling studies, I had already read and studied the work of Viktor Frankl, who, despite an appalling experience in a concentration camp, was able to find meaning in his existence in such a horrid place. He took control of his mind, thought of his beautiful memories, and dreamed about his future, all of which enabled him to survive.

I had already experienced how the flow of life would work for me when I let go, so I kept doing it. I kept letting go and surrendering to God. I had a deep faith that He was in control, and there was a greater purpose for me, so I kept trusting and dealt with whatever was put in front of me.

Meanwhile, I kept dreaming and believing that everything would continue to unfold. Why not keep dreaming? If I was going to fill my mind up with stuff, let them be dreams. So, I kept doing it, and truthfully, I still do it to this day.

Part VI

• Professional Greatness •

Chapter: 45

Just Keep Making the Next Right Move

A few weeks ago, my brother and I were discussing business, negotiations, and what it takes to make something happen. "Tarn, nothing is easy when it comes to business," he said to me.

My response was, yes, especially when you try to force something to happen and you know it doesn't quite fit. Then it can be very tough. During our conversation, I went on to add that whenever I let go of the reins, followed my deepest desires, and the flow of life, then everything worked out as it was supposed to.

This was exactly what happened when I was newly widowed. Even though I was creating my vision board and making plans, suddenly, without even trying, consulting clients were reaching out to me. I had a steady flow of work and some variety in my life. Once again, I was using my financial and computing skills, so it was a great boost to my personal and professional confidence after the previous year's events.

During this time, the world of coaching was evolving, and I instinctively knew to study toward being a personal and professional life coach. What then evolved was a steady clientele of private coaching clients. There was a nice mix, and I was fulfilled, and it all just naturally flowed.

The next step in following my heart was to write the book, publish the book, share it with the world, and commence speaking about my journey. Whilst it was still a dream in my heart, I had no idea how it would come about. I simply followed one step at a time and each step kept going in the right direction, until one day, I was holding not one, but two published books in my hand.

One of my consulting clients evolved over time into a full-time corporate role for a few years. What brought me the most joy about this client was not only the work, but also the fact that I was in the presence of people facing life-altering illnesses. This was what gave the role meaning and fed my sense of purpose. In my private life, I was also supporting people at the end stage of their lives or going through the cancer journey. Once again, I kept following my heart, making decisions, and then doing what was placed in front of me.

My decision to leave the corporate world was timely. I knew there was another book in me to be written, and my desire to help mankind on another level had to be explored. I didn't quite know what that looked like; however, I walked away from a secure financial package to step into the unknown. It was scary. But I knew to follow my bliss and what I believed would bring me a deeper sense of purpose.

This was a bold move for me. I'm a person who has had a high need for certainty and security. However, this decision was the beginning of many more bold moves, all in the name of purpose and meaning. I took the leap of faith, and as the saying goes, I trusted that the net would appear.

Coincidentally, at this time, I also attended my first Tony Robbins live event with Grant. We flew over to Australia to spend six days and nights immersed in personal development. Neither of us had ever done this before, and I was particularly excited to do it together with Grant. I had spent so much of my life on personal development, but for Grant, this was a very new experience.

Attending Date with Destiny had a major impact on us both, individually and together as a couple. For me, two major things happened. I removed from myself this incredibly heavy burden I carried about my parents, particularly my mother. Most of my life I had this belief that her happiness was my responsibility. It was during this event that I was able to finally release myself from this task and hand my beautiful mother over to God.

The other thing I let go of was Phil and my belief that I had to mourn him forever, to not truly move on with my life. I was able to finally let go of the remaining survivor's guilt that lingered and stopped me from being fully present in my life. I finally believed that I deserved to be happy again and gave myself permission to shine in life, in love, and professionally. I handed everyone, and everything else, over to God's hands.

What eventuated from Date with Destiny was my desire to level and upscale in several areas of my life and move my coaching business online. Grant and I attended Business Mastery in Las Vegas later that year where we experienced business teachings on a whole new level. Skills that I teach my clients today.

During this time, I engaged my own Tony Robbins coach for twelve months. She was an outstanding fit for me, and together we unravelled more of what needed to be inside of me. Just when I thought that all I needed was more strategy, I discovered that what I really needed was to let go of more deep pain, fear, grief, and poor decisions within me. This stuff held me back. I dealt with beliefs about why I was not good enough, why I couldn't do something, and why I continued to hold on to fear.

Within a month of our coaching, I declared that I wanted to become a Tony Robbins coach in time, and by February the following year, I found out that I was one of fifty applicants chosen amongst hundreds of other applicants around the world to begin the three-month interview process. It was three months I will never forget. I was tested in every possible way, and the experience was harder than anything else I have ever attempted or studied professionally.

I was given an education on resilience and coaching that was the most outstanding skill set I have ever gained professionally and given by some of the greatest coaches Tony himself had trained. In May of 2016, I was one of the successful twenty-five chosen from the final fifty applicants to be a Tony Robbins coach.

By the end of the training, I was tired, but, incredibly proud. I just kept following my heart, stepping out of my comfort zone, and taking the next right move.

During the following four years, I was an international online coach, and it all began by being a Robbins Coach. Gradually, private clients sought me out again, and eventually, I put my coaching programs online, which made coaching considerably easier. It enabled my clients to have all the materials they needed to work through things prior to each of our one-on-one sessions, so it was a win/win situation for us both.

Whilst I invested heavily in understanding the online world, funnels, sales, and everything else attached to it, what I always came back to was what my intuition already knew and felt comfortable with. There are so many strategies out there, ways of attracting your ideal clients, and inviting them to work with you. However, when I tried systems and methods that did not sit right with me or felt outside of my integrity and values, they never worked. I resisted the whole time.

What did work for me was letting go, trusting my instinct, knowing what my ultimate purpose and vision was, and acting accordingly. The more I let go, the more I was taken back to what I had believed in my heart from the very beginning. This then opened the right doors and allowed the right clients to find me in the right way, and they turned out to be perfect clients.

The same has happened when other doors were opened for me, whether they be media or other wonderful opportunities. Whenever I surrendered, let go, and let God, then amazing doors opened, ones that I could not have opened myself. Once a door was opened, I never hesitated and always walked through it. Each door I have walked through, even though in hindsight may not have taken me immediately where I thought it would, eventually led me down the right path.

During these past few years, and whilst I continued with my coaching, I also kept writing. Whether it be magazine articles or content for my book, writing filled my heart the most. I knew that this book would one day be complete, however, I also knew the timing wasn't quite right. Until now.

It was at the beginning of 2021 that I gave myself the time and space to do nothing but write. I serviced my existing clients, but I did not invite any more, as writing was my only focus. As I suspected, once making the decision to do nothing else but write, the words flowed.

Even though over the years I had written sixty-five thousand words of this book, I started again, and for the remaining three months, the words flowed. This is called doing what you love, and for now, being a writer is what I am loving.

Even though this was not how my journey began back in my university days, throughout the remainder of this part of the book, I will tell you more about how in making one decision after another, I found my way.

I will also share with you some of my own lessons about achievement, leadership, and finding my own definition of success.

Chapter: 46

From Accountant to Writer

The dream of writing a book was birthed within me, but I had no idea how the finished product would turn out. All I knew was to keep writing in my journal, day in and day out, and that somehow, those words would at least be a reminder of my own journey for when it came time to write the book.

Just prior to his diagnosis, Phil kept a journal, nothing personal, just all matter-of-fact leadership information and notes. Once he was diagnosed, his writing became deeper and more personal, and as he used to often say, it would one day make up his journey in the book.

So, I knew that I already had content, which was Phil's journey. I just had to prepare myself to read it. When I was ready, I commenced and underlined all the parts I knew would be perfect to tell some of his story.

I didn't commence my book for several months; however, I kept journaling. Then, one day, a colleague came to interview me as a subject for her own book that she was writing. By the end of our interview, she said to me, "Tanya, you must start writing this book. Your personal story and family life are too important not to share."

It was this prompting from her that gave me the kick I needed to at least start, so, in 2006, I started writing my first book. There was no title, just page after page of writing, which came straight from my heart.

The great thing was that I knew nothing about how to write a book. My sole intention was to share a story, leave a legacy for Phil and myself, and ultimately, help someone else along the way.

I had no idea how I would have it published, none. I did not think about marketing, but rather, I simply wrote the truth of what was in my heart at the time. It was uncomplicated and quite freeing to not have any other motives in mind when I wrote like that.

During the process of writing, I would have this dream in my mind of what it was going to feel like once my book was completed. I had this image in my mind, and the feeling of holding the finished product. I had no idea what was to be done between now and then, so I just kept writing. I never let go of how it was going to feel to hold this book in my hands. That kept me going and kept me writing.

Meanwhile, slowly I began doing homework on how to publish, spoke to some published authors, some past publishing computer clients, and other contacts. I wrote to publishers, submitted what was required, and did it all myself. It was quite a task, but I was determined. I had a very strong reason why this task was important to me, and I kept feeling that finished book in my hands.

To this day, whenever I need a prompt on the importance of never giving up on a dream, I think of this time. It wasn't easy, and I worked very hard at it. But I was determined and in love with my dream.

Knowing my books have helped others is important; however, one of the greatest things is that this entire process ignited in me a love of writing. A love that to this day, I can honestly say, brings me so much joy. Whether it is a book, an article, or even a post on social media, when I am present and flowing along with my emotions, so are the words. I have had the honour to have written thousands and thousands of words which have been published in various forms of media, and which I know have touched many lives. Tanya, the writer was born.

During his famous Stanford commencement address on June 12, 2005, Steve Jobs spoke about a quote that he read when he was seventeen that had a significant impact on his life. The quote went as follows: "If you live each day as if it were your last, someday you'll most certainly be right."

He went on to say that for the next thirty-three years he looked in the mirror and asked himself the question, "If today were to be the last day of my life, would I want to do what I am about to do today?" He decided that if his answer was no for too many days in a row, then he needed to change something, adding that remembering he would be dead soon was one of the most important tools he used to help him make the big choices in life.

Which is why, after my first books were published, I kept writing and have made the decision to complete this third book, and more beyond this one, no matter what.

My purpose for writing this piece on my transition to Tanya the writer is to encourage you to also keep dreaming, to reignite your professional dreams, to believe that you can have it, *if* you want it. So many people sadly give up too soon or let go of their dreams for whatever reason. Many believe it is too late, that they have missed the boat, that they are too old.

What if that was not true? What if all that needs to happen is that you be open to the possibility that what you really want for yourself is waiting for you? I invite you to be open to the possibility that there is still time, that you are still young enough, and that you can still have it.

Chapter: 47

From the Computer to the Stage

One day my mother said to me, "Tanya, you have got to make yourself happy." My response was to laugh out loud, because she was right. Not a truer word was spoken. Here she was, brought up in Yugoslavia without a college education, giving me the advice that many a famous teacher has written about for decades.

After my book *Unplanned Journey* was first published, I went on a tour of the United States and was asked by several television stations to appear and share my journey. As the requests started coming in and I was booking my flights, Mom said to me, "You know, Tanya, one day you might be interviewed by Dr. Robert Schuller on the Hour of Power." My response was, "Oh, Mom, that would be great. However, it is a bit of a big dream."

Quietly, despite my reserved response, I added that desire to my vision board as well! I began to visualise and feel what it would be like being interviewed by Dr. Schuller himself. After all, one of his famous quotes was, "What would you attempt if you knew you could not fail?"

Never underestimate the wisdom of our mamas and the power of holding on to your dream. In September of 2009, I was, in fact, on stage at the Crystal Cathedral in California, being interviewed by Dr. Robert Schuller about my book.

The experience of all those television interviews around the USA, then the finale of meeting Dr. Schuller, was a life experience that will always be embedded in my heart. Speaking so openly about my journey and how to overcome adversity was what I felt called to do, and here I was, doing it.

On my return to New Zealand, I was then invited to be the co-host of the Hour of Power on New Zealand Television, so once again, I was able to reach many people at once with a message of resilience and hope.

I could not help but think of that time in the kitchen when I heard God's voice and felt that there was a greater purpose for me amongst all this pain. I was reminded that you never quite know what is beyond the horizon, so I invite you to also keep going.

When I first felt the need to write and publish, I had no idea how to accomplish it. Thank goodness I didn't know what it would take. That alone would have stopped me many times, which is why I encourage you not to be overwhelmed by how you will attain your dream. Just know what your dream is, what your destination is, and if you can see only the first step, then take that.

Once you have taken that first step, then another will appear, and another, until, soon, the bigger picture will eventually unfold. Yes, some things do happen quickly, and people are at the right place at the right time for opportunities to show up. Many, however, take years and years to achieve their goals. Remember, it is not only about the outcome, but who you become in the process.

Even though it may feel like you are in limbo and it's uncomfortable right now, just ride it out, be patient, and take each step as it appears, never letting go of that big, bold dream of yours.

Chapter: 48

Authenticity, Integrity, and a Desire to Serve

My desire to become my own boss was strong in me from a very early age. I had no fear, and perhaps I was naïve. It just seemed like the natural thing to do, since my own father did so in his early forties, plus all my brothers eventually did as well.

One thing my parents taught me how to do was work, and I believe that's what instilled some of the boldness each time I took a leap of faith. My eagerness to commence my own business was so great that after completing my accountancy degree and doing my apprenticeship, even though I then landed an amazing corporate role with our national airline, I decided to quit it all at the age of twenty-seven and pursue my professional dream.

Everyone around me thought I had rocks in my head to leave such a steady job, one that could have had me going places within the airline. Yes, my move probably was a little silly, but I believed in myself.

What I had going for me was this naïve belief about life and business. Failure never entered my mind; it truly never occurred to me. I believed that what I was doing was right, and if I continued to work hard, I would reach my goal of being a self-employed businesswoman carrying a briefcase.

Whilst I probably didn't understand what authenticity and vulnerability meant back then, this is what I presented to the world. No pretences, no big promises, just me. This is who I am, and this is what I know I can do for you. So, are you prepared to hire me?

During the early weeks of being an entrepreneur, I knew nothing about sales, knowing who your ideal client was, or knowing how to market and attract them. I did some research, made one phone call, and from this one call came my first string of contract accounting jobs.

Not long after that, when MYOB accounting software was first introduced into New Zealand, I was in the right place at the right time, and from there began a successful career as an accounting software consultant. Once again, I just knew I needed to be authentic. I knew to keep working hard, and deep within me, I knew everything would be all right.

When I reflect on many of the decisions I have made in the past thirty years regarding my career, they were all that simple. My intention was always honesty; I presented my true, authentic self to a prospective client, showed my vulnerable side, and was prepared to laugh at myself when I goofed up. Then I fixed the problem, and this, I believe, is what people respected and why I built healthy professional relationships. I was also prepared to walk away in an instant if something felt off.

Some of my best decisions were those where money was not the major driver. What came first was purpose, how aligned a decision was with my values, and how this decision ultimately contributed to mankind. Not surprisingly, this work has always given me the greatest pleasure.

My goal was to always serve people, and if they became prospective clients from my genuine intention to serve, then great. If I knew I could help them, and they gave me the assurance they would do their part in creating change, then we were a great fit. If not, then I was always, always happy to walk away with my integrity intact.

To this day, this works for me, and clients who have come to me this way have been amazing and wonderful to work with. You start a relationship the way you want it to continue. Transparency, openness, and honesty will get you there every single time.

Chapter: 49

People Before Profits

One of the things that drives me nuts about my father, Smiley, is that he never stops talking. He also laughs all the time, at everything and everyone, including himself. The thing that I love about my father, and what everybody else loves about him, is that he never stops talking and laughing. Ask him to go to the grocery store for a couple of items, and two hours later you will be lucky to see him return. Everyone knew Smiley, and everyone loved Smiley.

People will always remember how they felt when they were in your company. They will always remember how you served them and the overall experience they had when they were your client. If the experience was great, they will share your name with a few people, but if they had a rubbish experience with you, they will tell everyone on the planet. Given the use of social media these days, it is highly likely they could. No matter what, the client experience is paramount.

Whether you are a business owner, a leader, or even an employee, it is your duty to always put the experience of your customer, your client, and your mentee as the highest priority.

Thankfully, I have a lot of my dad in me, and I love to talk and am genuinely interested in people. Most responded well to my curious nature. Therefore, we would build a healthy rapport that made it easy for me to show up for my clients, not only professionally, but also personally.

I always made myself available for my clients and was quite happy to extend the scope of service I provided. Without even knowing it, I became a mentor, confidante, counsellor, and coach, all without knowing that this would be part of my future and the bigger plan that had been set for me.

Whenever I demonstrated offering a computer software package to my clients, I always prayed beforehand and let go of the outcome on whether they would buy it or not. I simply trusted that the right decision would happen, and all I needed to demonstrate to my clients was that I would serve them no matter what.

My belief is that because of this trait, coming from a place of integrity, I never needed to do any marketing or selling. Everything flowed perfectly, and it was a rare occasion to experience difficulty with a client.

It was truly this simple, and what I have found is that today, in this modern world of fast-paced marketing, internet, and social media, the same principles apply. When I let go and trusted myself and God, then I met the right people at the right time, the right doors opened for me, and in my opinion, small miracles happened.

So long as I continue to operate from a place of personal authenticity and integrity, the flow of life happens, and the right clients come to me at the right time, just as it is meant to, for me and for them.

Every time I have tried to attract ideal clients by a means that felt uncomfortable to me, it did not work. Every time I focused only on the money, then my intention was off, and so was the result.

I share this as a reminder to keep it all simple. Be someone who will help influence or instill change into another human being. Be someone who will leave a positive impression with people so that they easily remember how they felt when in your company. You just may be the one person who helps them see their own potential. You may be the one person who encourages them to dig deep and find their own superhero.

Just as that wonderful elderly couple shared with me as a teenager, the lesson is that honesty, integrity, authenticity, and respect for another, in every area of your life, will always come back and reward you.

What has also always worked for me is to come back to what I believe is my core purpose in life, my divine mission, and then everything else simply flows.

My clients became more than my computer clients. Soon, whilst sitting beside them at their office desk, I became their confidante. Soon, they would reach out to me in between our professional visits, and, when appropriate, I would help them. I even sat with some as they lived out their final days.

This desire to go over and above for your client, to place people before profits, was what I believe helped me not only in business, but also in life. You just never quite know what the bigger picture has in store for you when your simple intention is to serve a fellow human being.

Chapter: 50

Abundant to the Core

One of the greatest lessons from my parents was the willingness and discipline of knowing how to work, and, when necessary, how to work hard. Being the youngest and only girl, I spent the most time with my mom, and the additional lesson I learned from her when it came to money was how to save and respect money.

Thanks to Mom, my parents were mortgage-free in their early forties, back in the days when mortgage interest rates were in the high double digits. She was wise, she knew how to make money stretch, and she learned how to not give money to others for something she could do herself.

The gift I received from my dad was how to enjoy money and live in the present moment. Sometimes I think he really believed money grew on trees, as he certainly knew how to enjoy it and always had this belief that more would miraculously appear.

Whilst I observed both, thankfully, I preferred the more cautious approach from Mom, which enabled me to maintain a more balanced and conservative relationship with money. It did not, however, stop me from going without, as I have always enjoyed nice things.

So, I grew up knowing money, liking it, enjoying earning it, watching my bank balance grow, and not feeling that I had to spend it all when it came in.

Having the eating issues was a blessing when it came to money, because, in a way, food and money were the same. I learned that buying a lot of nothing, just like eating a lot, was a temporary fix to ease my pain. One of my greatest lessons was that when I was down or low, spending would never be a long-term solution to feeling better.

I felt so proud when I landed my first job in a department store at fourteen years of age. I wasn't so cocky by the end of my first week when my boss pulled me aside and informed me that I had short-changed my customers by a total of fifty-two dollars, which, back in 1978, was big money.

Soon I got the hang of it, and, over time, I felt proud that, at such an early age, I understood the value of working hard and saving. I enjoyed the independence that earning my own money gave me, and I grew to respect how hard my parents had to work for their money as well. I also learned how to be smart with money, be disciplined with it, and develop a healthy relationship with money.

Even though I was on the cautious side when it came to taking risks with money, my desire for freedom was always there. Trusting myself when it came to money and my ability to go out and earn it has played a major part in my future and ability to keep dreaming. It also played a major part in knowing and believing I would always be taken care of and trust that life would always come through for me, as it always did, and continues to do so.

So, I experienced, from a very early age what it was like to have a healthy bank balance from hard work and saving. It helped me not to fear money or feel guilty for having it, but to really like it, without having a destructive, unhealthy attachment to it.

This basic knowledge, discipline, and respect for money have been an incredible asset all my life, especially later when I was single. I felt in control of my own finances and never felt the need to rely on anyone else to manage them. In fact, I have always managed my own business finances, and, to this day, manage our joint finances, because I feel competent at it.

Not everyone is the same. Many people who are single fall into the trap of not taking care of their own finances and become victims of scammers, lovers, or predators who specifically target the vulnerable. I cannot say this enough: if your relationship with money is not healthy, if you find yourself with what many refer to as a "scarcity mindset," then I encourage you to have the courage to examine your financial habits and change them accordingly.

If you continue to spend more than you can realistically afford, then ask yourself why. What else is going on? If you always trust others with your money and not your own instinct, then develop that internal muscle. If you are overspending on others, or if you feel that you are being taken for granted in a new relationship, then do something about it.

You may not feel confident enough to speak up about it, however, I cannot encourage you enough, as this is a common problem for many. Now is the time to let go of any shame you may be carrying and face your financial reality.

Also, if you feel that you are spending excessively because of your grief or loneliness, then speak to someone, and get the help you need. If you do not want to spend the money on yourself to get help, then work out how much it is going to cost you financially in twelve months if you do *not* fix this!

It is so common to put your head in the sand when it comes to money, and I encourage you to look at it, as there are so many ways you can waste or lose it.

Also, if you have had bad experiences with money in the past and it takes you to a place of being a victim to finances, then perhaps it is also time to sort this out. Perhaps you do not want to have financial wealth because of what everyone will think of you. I encourage you to get over that fear, too. If you have a belief that you will never have money or that you will always be poor, then chances are you will be.

It's okay to have money. It's the unhealthy attachment, behaviours, or relationship to money that can trip you up and have long-lasting, often devastating results. Again, if reading this is making you squirm, then I invite you to look deeper.

One of the things that has always helped me in this area is to remember that money is temporary, given to me on loan. When I take my final breath, none of my wealth will be coming with me!

Chapter: 51

Knowing Your Professional Worth

At sixteen, I walked into my first therapy session, paid for by me, without anyone else knowing. At eighteen, I walked into my first twelve-step meeting. By the time I was twenty, I completed my three-year bachelor's degree at Auckland University, followed by two years of hard practical experience to be admitted to the New Zealand Institute of Chartered Accountants.

Since then, I have spent another five years of study toward various other diplomas and qualifications, not to mention the hours of training as a Tony Robbins coach.

The monetary cost of all my study, courses, seminars, business consultants, therapists, and coaches over the years would most definitely be in the hundreds of thousands of dollars, and every penny was worth its weight in gold.

All the above is only the education component of my curriculum vitae; it does not include the fifty years of my life experiences, only a handful of which I've written about in this book.

So, if ever you are questioning your professional worth, then I invite you to reflect on everything you have been through in life, and every investment you have made in your personal development, over and above your educational and professional accomplishments.

When I think about the value I have given to my clients, whether employers or business clients, it has nothing to do with an hourly rate. My worth to a client or a business colleague is not something that can be measured by time, but rather the outcome I can help my client achieve.

In many cases, particularly in the kind of work I do, the outcome is not always measurable in financial terms. How can you place a value on your health, your life, your marriage, your ability to become unstuck, and finally feel good about who you are and the direction you are going in?

It is not about what it will cost you to make a change in your life; it is about what it will cost you not to make a change. So, if someone questions the cost in working with me, once again, it is about asking the question of what it is going to cost you by *not* working with me.

This way of thinking can be translated over several areas of life, especially in your professional life. So often, we do not value our contribution, so we undercharge, we get used by others, and build resentment in our professional life.

One of the gifts of aging is finally understanding your true worth, even when it comes to your professional greatness. I wonder how many days I wasted worrying about what people thought about me. I wonder how many days I played small because I didn't want to appear "too much" for others. I wonder how many days I wanted and waited for others to show me that I was enough. I wonder how many hours I worked for next to nothing because I didn't believe I deserved to be paid what I was worth.

It took me some time to fully understand and put this way of thinking into practice, and it is one I invite you to also think about and explore as well. No matter what professional relationship you are in, everything I have written about worth, respect, and identity applies here as well.

As the saying goes, if I do a job in thirty minutes, it's because I spent forty years learning how to do that job in thirty minutes. You owe me for the years of experience, not the minutes.

Chapter: 52

D is for Discipline!

Do you remember when, as a child, we would play the game of hide-and-seek and believe that by covering our eyes and not being able to see others, they could not see us? As adults, we close our eyes to some of our own behaviours and bad habits, pretending they are not happening because we are the only ones who can see them, so they don't count.

Then, we work with employees, colleagues, or clients and expect them to do what we know we are not doing ourselves, which then leads to our own inner turmoil and shame.

As the saying goes, how you do one thing is how you do everything, so, if we are going to be an example to others and share guidelines with others on how to stop certain behaviours, then it is our duty to start in our own camp first.

One of the areas of life I wanted to be an example in was discipline. Sometimes, it is not easy and takes real grit. Life continues to bring challenges, and all we want to do is have another drink or pull up a chair at the refrigerator and eat everything in sight.

We must learn to say no to ourselves, to say, "I will not do this anymore. This is no longer who I am." Whilst it can be difficult to do, over time each "no" becomes easier to say, until one day, before you know it, the pattern will be broken.

The reason why so many great teachers preach about the importance of living one day at a time is because this is the best way to live life, especially when you are faced with adversity. Take one day at a time, twenty-four hours, and then, when it is done, you awake the following day and do it all again.

Taking ownership of your life and happiness is one of the most empowering decisions you can make, just as being a leader means leading by example and practicing what you preach. Without self-discipline, you cannot authentically expect it from your peers or direct circle.

If you are an executive in a corporation and expect accountability, time management, and responsibility from your staff, then this is what you must also practice, even when no one else is looking! If you are a thought leader, coach, or in the helping profession, it is about practicing what you teach others and being a true leader.

No matter how high your position in life or profession, we are all human, and there is no shame in admitting that you have some issues to address. Whether they be physical or emotional habits, we all have stuff to deal with at some stage in our lives. It may be that your first step is accepting that, for you, this is okay. Many carry this belief that unless they appear perfect to the world, then they are flawed. I invite you to get over it.

It may also mean letting go of this belief that things will just disappear or sort themselves out on their own if we just close our eyes. They may diminish for a while but reappear when we are triggered. Then we find ourselves repeating the same pattern, regaining the same pounds, or raising our voices in the same tone, even after we declared to the world we never would again.

Have you ever felt relieved when you held something inside, then realised you were not the only one who felt or behaved in the same way? This is the relief I want you to experience when I say that, whatever it is you hide from the world, it is highly likely you are not the only person who feels the same way.

Without question, lasting change takes a decision; it takes motivation, commitment, and discipline. Do not let this stop you from showing up as the professional powerhouse you were meant to be. The world needs you, needs your message, and needs your experience. Own it, and just do it.

Part VII

• Spirituality •

The Foundation Beneath Everything

Chapter: 53

The Winning Ticket

The raffle ticket cost me two cents. At the age of five, this was to be my first flutter at gambling, and it was to be my first win. I remember proudly buying the ticket with my own money one Sunday after church. First prize was a picture of Jesus surrounded by the apostles at the Last Supper. The picture was stuck on a piece of cardboard, and the edges of the cardboard had a border made of wool, all woven like a spiral-bound book.

Words on a page cannot express how good it felt to win this image. I loved it, as I loved anything else to do with God, Jesus, Mary, or all those other robed people up there in the sky with them. I didn't quite know why I loved them so much, I just did. I especially loved to visit my parents' elderly friends, some of whom were very religious, and had pictures of all these people, plus angels, scattered around their homes.

Even though my parents were brought up in a communist country, they were both raised in very religious Catholic homes. My Baba, my grandmother on my mother's side, took her final breaths clutching her rosary beads. She used to keep her stash of dinar in her Catholic calendar and knew how much was tucked away within the pages of each month. Her faith was simple, yet strong, as was my mother's.

Also raised in the Catholic faith, I went to a Catholic school until I was eight years of age. Once we moved from the country into the city, I couldn't settle and was moved to a public, non-religious school. Whilst we all went to Mass on Sunday and prayed grace occasionally, my loveliest memories were of Mom saying our evening prayers by our bedside, usually in her native tongue. I would then carry on praying in bed, and this nightly ritual has continued to this day.

My intention for this part of the book is not to talk about religion. It is to talk about my personal path to God. Without this journey, I know that I would not be who I am today, nor would I have the courage to write this book.

Many have come to me for help in life because they know of my simple but strong belief in God, and they, too, are searching. My deepest desire is to help a fellow human being on their own journey back to that deeper place they are searching for. Many still don't even know what that looks like.

One of the gifts of studying to be a therapist is that you learn the art of respecting other people's beliefs and their model of the world. I have had the most wonderful coaching relationships with beautiful people from a variety of different cultures and religious beliefs, and I have loved every moment of it. For those who were on a spiritual journey, my intention has always been simple, to help them find clarity on what spirituality even means, and then to walk beside them as they find their own path.

Whether it is referred to as God, spirituality, faith, peace, consciousness, or whatever other term might be used out there to describe your longing, then hopefully my journey to God, as written in these pages, will assist you on your search.

When I commenced writing this book, I still didn't know how deeply I would share about my own spiritual journey and the impact it has had on my life. The more I wrote, the more certain and important it became to share my story unashamedly. Without the telling of my journey, I would be leaving out a big part of the story and the foundation of how I have travelled the road from grief to greatness.

My faith has always been simple. I never doubted the existence of God; I just knew He was there. That is still the truth about my faith today, and, in a nutshell, it has been the biggest component of how I have overcome adversity. I am intentionally selective about how and when I share my faith and find that this is what has worked best for me and others. Once I am asked, though, I share openly. To hide my faith would be a disservice to mankind!

Ever since I was a little girl, I have always had a strong connection and devotion to Mary, the mother of Jesus. Majka Božija, my mother would refer to her during our nightly prayers. This devotion has continued throughout my lifetime, and once I learned of the apparitions in Medjugorje, a small village only a forty-five-minute drive from my mother's, I had to go and have returned many times since.

Even whilst growing up, I would attend Mass with my parents. I wasn't present, and truthfully, was slightly rebellious. I didn't listen much at all to religious studies, so much so that I didn't even realise I was having my first confession until one day I found myself in the confessional.

As a teenager, during Mass, I would sneak my handwritten notes into church and use it as a time to memorise my notes in preparation for my exams. I wasn't one for rules and didn't listen to what anyone said, however, I still believed and prayed and knew I was being heard by God. Many have told me that I am the most rebellious Catholic they know. What draws them to me, however, is this simple, blind faith in God.

Walking into my first twelve-step meeting at eighteen years of age was my first experience of being around other people with a different faith or belief in God. Many would talk about their higher power, something greater than themselves, which I found rather refreshing.

Many of my friends were great believers in God; however, they were not Catholic. This I found incredibly helpful and a wonderful way for me to experience how other people lived out their faith. I happily attended Baptist, Anglican, home groups, and more, in addition to going to a Catholic Mass. I loved them all.

So, thankfully, my eyes were opened and my ability to see how differences in beliefs need not get in the way when, as humans, we unite. We were all on a journey, wanting the same outcome, but we all took a slightly different path to get there. For me, that was okay.

The journey was about searching for what felt right for me, what I felt the most aligned with, and to finding my own definition of faith without rules, regulations, shame, or guilt.

During my tumultuous twenties, I wasn't attending Mass much at all, perhaps just on big occasions. Even though I was in deep pain, I was also incredibly close to God. I regularly read my Bible; I had friends who were very close to God; and I relied on quiet time with God to get me through. I just followed my path, knowing I would find my way.

It was my devotion to Our Lady Mary, plus my absolute love of being in a Catholic Church and attending a Mass with meaning, that I couldn't help but love. Whilst I went on a bit of a search, it was not until I was thirty that I had made the conscious decision to return to regular Catholic Mass.

My aunt had given me a book about Medjugorje and the apparitions of Our Lady in the former Yugoslavia. Even though I regularly prayed, it was after reading this book that I developed a deep knowing within that I needed to return to regular Mass.

Whilst I have had incredible things happen to me during my life, once I devoted myself to God again and made His will for me the most important thing in my life, extraordinary events have happened. Yes, many of them heartbreaking and grief that I would not wish upon anyone; however, there have also been many miracles.

Without question, my walk with God has been my answer in every area of my life, my struggles with self-worth, my food issues, overcoming grief, my professional life, and even my relationships with people. Every area of my life has been enriched and fulfilling because of my belief in God, that He is always listening, and His will for my life is my answer to everything.

Despite my rebellion and the need to define what faith and spirituality meant for me, I had to do it this way. It was, and still is, a deep spiritual journey back to finding me in the process. What I do know is that with God by my side, I have a deep certainty that I can handle anything that life hands to me.

This was my way, and my wish for you is that this part of the book may also help you find clarity and the road that feels right for you.

Chapter: 54

God Was My Mate from the Beginning

I can still remember standing at the start line of the one-hundred-yard girls' final of our primary school sports day. At the age of ten, even though I had already proven myself to be a fast sprinter, I had not yet won any major races, so was never known as the best, more like in the top five.

On this day, however, I felt like the fastest. I recall standing at the start line, feeling nervous, and praying. I asked God to be with me for every step and to help me win. I felt on top of the world. I felt grown-up, and I knew I had it in me to win. A feeling of confidence rose within me, as if no one else existed on the field, just me and God.

Preparing to pounce once the start gun went off, my final act was to cross my fingers on both hands as I waited. Then *bang*, the start gun went off. I took off like a bird and ran with every bit of everything inside me. I felt like a bullet racing down the grassed track, as if something was carrying me.

With my fingers still crossed on both hands, I was the first to cross the finish line and was crowned the fastest girl in school. No one expected me to win, not even me, until I got to the start line and decided that, with God's help, I could.

Growing up, people were shocked when I would tell them about my low self-worth as a youngster and how it still lingered in the background of my mind. Despite the self-doubt inside and the food issues, it never stopped me from trying something new.

Alongside competing in sporting events, I would also sing on stage, solo, duets, quartets, and in groups. I was what many would call an extrovert, not at all shy to put myself out there in the public eye. I tied this boldness to the simple faith my mother had taught me, that God and Our Lady would always protect me and be beside me, no matter what I did in life.

Even though my parents endured extraordinary hardships, never did I ever hear them chastise or blame God. They had endured, demonstrated resilience, and prayed they would be given the strength to get through.

When I am asked how it is that I always appear so self-assured and confident, apart from sharing about the forty-odd years of personal development, I always add that my simple belief in a loving God helps me through any trial, even my self-worth.

It was also what Dr. Robert Schuller shared with me during our meeting together. Both he and Dr. Viktor Frankl believed that everything in our lives was determined by our own level of self-worth. The way you feel about yourself will determine how you feel about others, how you feel about life, and will ultimately be the barometer for the quality of your life.

The twelve-step program helped me a lot when it came to building a strong personal foundation. It reminded me daily of the importance of relying on a higher power and of living one day at a time. Combining these two strategies was a turning point for me when it came to having a deep acceptance of self.

For a very long time, I felt deeply flawed, broken, and different, and this was what I needed to change. These thoughts drove me to binge on food, make bad choices, and suffer deep unhappiness. I learned to take my problems to God every day in my daily prayers. I discovered prayer worked.

Each day, I would say something along the lines of, "*God, I am asking that somehow you miraculously help me love and accept myself. Help me to feel just a bit of how much you love me.*"

When I truly let go and believed that what I asked would be given to me, it was. This simple daily prayer was what worked for me to build a deep respect and acceptance of self. The trick was to remember to do it every day, until it became part of my daily prayer, until it became a habit, until it became a part of who I was.

Another strategy I used was to write out my prayers, like the prayer above. From a very early age, I would write out all the reasons why I was worthy, why I was lovable, and why I was enough. I kept remembering that God loved me, and this was a great start. I made the writing a ritual, using a beautiful journal, as well as a nice pen. Seeing it handwritten was always considerably more powerful than typing it out on a keyboard.

Whether you believe in God, in a higher power, the Universe, or any other higher being, if this is something that resonates with you, then I encourage you to try it. This simple technique has worked for me for decades, and still does, whenever I need reminding that I am enough.

Chapter: 55

God Showed Me When to Love and When to Let Go

A businesswoman whom I respect greatly once said to me, "Never burn your bridges with anyone. Don't make enemies. Don't allow yourself to react in such a way that you will regret those words later. Keep all your doors open. You never quite know what or who life has lined up for you, so, as much as you want to be right, if you can, practice the pause and zip it."

One of the sayings I heard Tony Robbins say a few years ago was "Choose your friends, love your family." We all have had difficult friendships and relationships with our family. Sometimes, friendships or intimate relationships must end for one reason or another. They hurt at the time. You don't want to feel the discomfort. You want to let them know how much you're hurting, or maybe you want to hold on to the ill feeling toward them. However, there is another way.

It was from the Bible and from the twelve-step program that I learned to pray for those whom I had difficulty with. Whilst, at times, I felt I wanted to throw up in my mouth instead of praying for someone who had hurt me, I would still try, because I knew that praying for them brought me relief. Those times when I was defiant and rebelled, I would then ask God to give me the willingness to be willing to open my mouth and at least try and utter something that resembled a prayer for someone who had hurt me.

Now it comes easier. I know that this is the fastest and most effective way to release myself from the head crazies. People will always be people. People will always say and do stupid things, and, at times, hurtful things. It has happened from the beginning of time, and it will continue to happen.

Some of these people will be in our lives for a very long time, and, whilst we cannot expect them to change, what we can do is love them, let them be who they are, and not react to their actions and words. If you do, then immediately let them go, leave them in God's hands, and even ask God to remove your frustration, hurt, anger, sadness, and whatever it may be that you feel toward them.

We cannot control or change others. What we can do is hand them over to God and ask Him to take care of them, to change them if they need to be changed. We know how tough it is to take ownership of our own lives, admit to our mistakes, and make changes, so everyone else must be given the same privilege to see something for themselves. It is not up to us to shove our opinions in their face, telling them what they should be doing.

We have the gift of knowing how to let go and not let anything or anyone disturb our peace of mind. Our anger and resentment, should we choose to hold on to those feelings, is no one else's fault but our own. We choose those emotions.

If you are reading this and your teeth are clenching, or you are feeling some sort of discomfort about another human being, I invite you to pray and let it go. If you are not willing to let it go, then pray to be willing to let it go. Nothing is worth messing up your day or your mind.

The biggest gift that we have, yet do not use, is to leave others in the hands of God, and release them from our own hands, especially those who are in our lives regularly. It is said that there is no need to cut people off if you don't want to, or if you are not yet ready to, just continue to grow, keep praying for them, and eventually they just fall off if they are meant to.

Meanwhile, always have an honest intention, keep praying for them, and for yourself, that you do the right thing.

Chapter: 56

Grief, God, and Surrender

I was sitting in the front pew with my parish priest, Monsignor Cronin, the day after Phil's diagnosis, crying. Mons held my hand, and as we both looked up at Jesus on the cross, he gently whispered to me, "Whatever His will." They were not unlike Phil's own words five months later, only two hours prior to his death. Whilst looking at the image of Jesus on the wall at the end of his bed, he said to me, "Tarn, whatever He wants."

Someone once said to me that grief is like a fingerprint; it is different for us all. Which is why the story I share is my personal story, some of which you may relate to, some of which you may not. I would not be sharing my truth if I did not share with you the role that my faith has played in helping me to deal with loss.

Grief and loss can be crippling. If I was to share with you how I deal with loss in a couple of words, it would be acceptance and God. When I am unable to find it in me to accept whatever is happening in my life, then I call on God.

My daily mantra, which I would speak out loud or listen to, included the following line: "*There is no task too great, nor problem too heavy, that I cannot handle.*" I developed a deep belief that, with the help of God, there was no problem or feeling I couldn't face, feel, or sit with.

I would also go back and read many short phrases of the Bible that gave me strength during times of great suffering. "*So, if you are suffering according to God's will, keep on doing what is right and trust yourself to the God who made you, for He will never fail you.*" 1 Peter 4:19, (*Life Application Bible*, 1988).

Sometimes I would talk to Phil and say, "You know, I know you are feeling joy and happiness right now. Help me to also feel the slightest amount of joy and happiness that you are feeling right now. Help me to get through this one day by experiencing joy and knowing you are near."

When I remembered to do this, every single time I asked, the grief began to dissipate, and slowly the peace came. There are so many other instances like this documented in my first book, *Unplanned Journey*, when during my darkest moments, my prayers were always answered.

What I do know is that grief and sorrow will always be present in life, as will happiness, joy, and laughter. I finally understood that it didn't need to be one or the other, that all those emotions could exist together, and it was okay.

My God is a loving God, who also wants us to be joyful and live a life of fulfilment and abundance. I believed that God wanted me to rise and shine and live my one precious life, so I did.

Chapter: 57

Lost and Found

"The house is flooding!" were the screaming words from Grant that awoke me at approximately 2:15 a.m. on that night in early June 2017. I was immediately wide awake, and as soon as I turned the corner out of our bedroom, the lights were on, and I could see the cascade of water pouring through the top floor of our home.

Grant raced around trying to find the source of the water, which he did very quickly. A freak accident from our kitchen taps created a flood that, over the next few weeks, we would discover destroyed most of our beautiful new home.

Six months earlier, we made the bold decision to buy a beach house an hour and a half from the city. It was a brave move financially, but we followed our instinct and allowed the flow of life to take over. If it was meant to be, it would be. Well, it turned out to be.

Soon after our decision, we found a large home on the beach, one that needed a bit of cosmetic work. Once it was fixed up, we knew it would be nice. It was a great financial decision, and whilst it stretched us, we knew we had to buy it. Everything fell into place to make it happen. It was a wonderful home to take care of our elderly parents because it was so large. Each had their own room.

I won't deny that my first impression on seeing the house wasn't great. It looked a mess. My first words were, "I am not going to live in this!" However, I soon changed my mind after I looked beyond the disrepair. I felt deeply that if everything happened easily for us, then to flow with it.

For so long, I had wanted the peace and space to write my next book, and this would be the perfect environment to do it in. We would live there for twelve months full-time and then decide what to do with the house after that. Once we took possession in April, the painting and recarpeting began, and within weeks, we moved in for our twelve-month adventure at the beach.

It was a big move for me. I was truly stepping out of my comfort zone, but it felt so right. We found the perfect tenants for our city home, the move went smoothly, my cat Fergus loved it, and we also loved the peace and quiet. We had no doubt that God was walking beside us on our adventure.

The following six weeks felt like peaceful bliss. Grant commuted to work; I took my time unpacking; and then I began to write so freely, enjoying the beach and the peace and calm that came with it. I felt so close to God and embraced the opportunity to slow down my mind, write, and bask in that peace that I had so longed for.

It was the perfect home for my parents to visit, and for those six weeks, they came three times to stay for the weekend. We cooked, fished, and enjoyed our time together.

On that night in June 2017, Grant and I fell into bed at 9:30 p.m., exhausted. It had been a big day. My parents were staying overnight; the boys had gone out fishing; and we finally finished unpacking. Grant had put up the last mirror and assembled our infrared sauna. Then, five hours later, Grant awoke to the sound of water, and I to the sound of his yelling.

We spent a few hours that night going through this massive home trying to clean up the mess and assess the damage. Despite the lower level looking like a waterfall through each light socket, we still didn't realise the extent of the damage.

The following morning, as we were taking everything out of the house again and storing it in our garage, the sorrow hit me. Grant held me as I wept, feeling the loss, without realising the reality of what lay ahead for us.

I felt so sad for us. It was our first home together, and we loved it. The first six weeks were magical. We were so happy I couldn't believe it, and now it had come to an end. I had to muster up every ounce of strength in me to not fall into the abyss of depression and my old belief that joy would never last for me.

It was a story that I had to change when Phil was diagnosed, and I could not help but feel that here I was again, going through loss with Grant.

Standing in the garage that morning with my husband, with all our soaked possessions around us, I could not help but think of the time when I first witnessed the same kind of loss in my parents' eyes when our home burned to the ground.

My childhood memory of losing our house kept going through my mind that day of the flood. If my parents got through a much bigger, devastating loss, then I could get through this. After all, what we lost was just stuff, and as Mom and Dad had rebuilt everything they needed again, so could we.

Grant and I remained in shock, though. It was several weeks before we discovered that the house was destroyed far more completely than we could see. For the next six months, I became an onsite project manager to oversee the repair, and Grant continued his commute to the city to work.

Most of the time, we lived in and endured the mess. Our tolerance and faith were tested as never before, and then, two weeks after the project was complete and we moved back in, my cat of sixteen years, Fergus, suddenly died. His death tipped me over the edge, and I fell on my knees to ask for God's sustenance through this grief.

The book I had been writing was placed on hold. Soon, I realised there was more to my story than I originally thought. Instead of writing about my life, I was still living it.

A few days after Fergus passed away, Grant and I were lying in bed. Weeping, I asked my husband, "Why do you think everything that has happened to us over the past six months has happened?"

"Good question," was Grant's response. "We will just have to wait and see."

What got us through was the same as what had always gotten us through. Acceptance and a deep belief that this was all part of a bigger plan for us. We had no idea what it would look like. We simply trusted that there would be a silver lining someday. Meanwhile, every time we felt the stress, anger, and frustration of our circumstances, we would come back to our faith and know that perhaps our lives and my book needed another chapter on resilience.

The journey with our home was a big lesson about letting go of the material loss and discovering what we found in the process. During this time, my relationship with Grant strengthened to a level that it would not have had we not had the flood. We both developed a level of resilience and faith that may not have happened had it not been for the flood. I felt a deeper level of commitment to Grant and our life together, letting go more of the sorrow of my past and embracing the wonderful now.

We ended up selling our dream home a couple of years later. The flow of life worked in such a way that the perfect people bought it. Whilst this journey ended differently than how we had originally imagined it, the synchronicity and magical God moments and lessons that happened for us were priceless. What we gained far outweighed what we had lost.

There was no way in the world we could have planned or orchestrated the events that occurred during that time. There are too many to write about. I have kept a special diary of God's magical moments in my life, and this period at the beach blew our minds. Grant felt the same way.

Eventually, we returned to our home in the city, and ever since, we have trusted God without reservation. He has proved to us that what is beyond the horizon, out of sight, is as it is meant to be.

Chapter: 58

Handing Everything Over

Florida. It was during my training to be a Tony Robbins coach. I had been awake for almost twenty-four hours. It was 11:00 p.m., and everyone was really excited about the highlight of the day, walking on hot coals of fire. Not me. I was an overtired, crazy woman and wanted nothing to do with it. I was on the phone to my husband in New Zealand, asking about the fastest way to get out of there.

Whilst I was still breathing, there was no way I would be walking on hot coals that night. All I wanted was to go to bed. My lovely husband Grant just listened and encouraged me the best he could. With nothing he could do, he just listened and attempted to calm me down.

We hung up our phone call, and I began to wander through the crowds of hundreds and hundreds of people all about to do what they had been waiting all night to do. The excitement was clearly contagious. Suddenly, something inside me changed. To this day I cannot tell you where the spark came from. It was in that moment I made the decision to do the fire walk.

I had no idea what to do. I hadn't listened to any of the instructions. I stepped into a line outside in the dark, and coincidentally, I found one of my friends. By the time we got to the **front** of the queue, I could see the flaming coals and looked over to my friend and asked, "What are we supposed to do? I wasn't listening." I am not sure how he responded, but what I do remember is looking up, praying, and placing myself in an indestructible state of certainty as I took hold of God's hand and walked over those coals as if I was walking on air. I got to the end feeling as though it was the simplest thing to do in my life. There was not a mark on my feet, and I was on such a high because I felt the presence of God with me like I hadn't for a very long time. I truly felt He carried me. What excited me the most was how I experienced going from a state of absolute craziness a few minutes earlier, to now one of absolute joy, and it all happened like the flick of a switch.

One thing I have discovered over the years is that no problem is too big for God, and no problem is too small. God is always with us whether we are trying to cope with the depths of pain that accompanies grief; trying to solve a problem at work or with finances; asking Him to help us walk over hot coals; or even something as basic as how much food to put in our mouths. When we fully surrender, ask for a solution, and trust that it will be the right one, He answers and shows us the way.

When someone asks me how I managed to overcome my food problem and look so well all the time, I simply say, "I gave up." I took my hands off the steering wheel and gave up, everything. Dieting, counting calories, restricting, watching food groups, or the latest fad diets. I could no longer be bothered, and if it meant that at times I was not eating a balanced meal, I didn't care. So long as I wasn't obsessing or binging.

At times I was so over this food issue that I would simply fall on my knees and say, God, you take this. You remove from me this obsession with food, calories, diets, my weight, everything. Take it! Then often I would add, just for today, as I knew that if I felt the freedom just for one day, then I could repeat it again the following day.

With this crazy food thing, sometimes you get to the point where you not only don't know how much to eat anymore, but you also don't even know what to eat anymore. You completely lose sight of what you enjoy, what your taste buds enjoy, what you crave.

Hence, it was not uncommon for me to also ask; You know what, God? I have no idea what to eat anymore. I have no idea what I like, and I have no idea how much, so I let go of that too. Please, I ask you to monitor my appetite and my food choices. Help me this way to learn what I like, what I don't like, how much is enough for my body, and how much is excess.

When it comes to my daily health, my motivation to be well and remain well, the most important part of the equation to getting it all right is still prayer and my trust in God. When do I do it? Whenever I think of it during the day. As this has been part of my routine and habit for decades now, it comes naturally, however, I pray and reach out whenever I need to. For me it is important to not have rigid rules, even if I make them myself, because I am sure to rebel and break them.

The other thing I totally left in God's hands was money and my relationship to it. I just kept handing it over, clearing my beliefs, and trusting that all would be taken care of. I had a simple belief that so long as I did not have an unhealthy attachment to money, and that I was generous with it, God would always supply what I needed. There were many times in my life when I felt totally taken care of financially and professionally. Opportunities and money came my way that I could not have dreamed possible. In fact, those words also soon became my daily gratitude prayer. I am grateful and worthy of the unlimited abundance that will today and every day continue to flow to me and through me. Opportunities and money will come to me that I could not have dreamed possible.

I have a written diary of every single financial and professional miracle that has come my way. There is no way I could have planned or orchestrated these events. They were truly divine. Having them documented is always a wonderful way to remember that God has His hand on everything, even my bank account and professional opportunities.

Another line in my daily prayer is **There is no client who will come to me that I cannot help. Everything I do today will contribute to the greater good of humanity. Every person with whom I have contact today will be served in some way by me.**

I also trusted God as my CEO and organiser of my diary. Many times, I often feel drained and depleted, so I reboot, rejuvenate, and always remember one of my favourite quotes in the Bible. As it says in 1 Chronicles 28:20, "Be strong and courageous and get to work. Don't be frightened by the size of the task, for the Lord my God is with you, He will not forsake you. He will see to it that everything is finished correctly." (Life Application Bible, 1988)

Put everything in God's hands. Everything! Whatever your spiritual belief, whomever it is you talk to and pray to, then I invite you to talk and pray more. Let go of everything. If you are walking down a set of stairs carrying a load of something, say, Thank you, God, for helping me get down the stairs safely.

If you are riding your scooter, your pushbike, or your skateboard, thank God for keeping you safe.

If you are about to go into a meeting and want a specific result, thank God that you get the outcome you are looking for.

If you want to sell your home for a certain price, thank God for bringing you the perfect buyers with the perfect price.

If you want to reach a certain financial result in your business or in your savings, thank God in advance for reaching that goal by the mentioned date.

If you are ready for love, thank God for helping you to be prepared for love, to be ready to allow it, and to notice the right person when they are brought into your life.

If you are feeling emotionally fragile, ask God to help you notice the beauty around you, or within you, that you are missing.

If you are ready to forgive someone, however, you are not quite willing yet, then thank God for the willingness to be willing to forgive them.

If you are ready to fall asleep peacefully and find you are still awake, then pray, and thank God for everything you have in your life. Hand everything over. It truly is as simple as that.

Chapter: 59

Choosing Faith Over Fear in a Pandemic

We flew out to the United States for our planned holiday on the exact day Covid-19 had its first case arrive in New Zealand. Despite a family member saying we were mad in going, it didn't enter our minds not to go.

We freely travelled around the United States, being careful with our own health, believing that we would be safe and free of all illness. We attended a conference with about two hundred people in close proximity to everyone and continued to hold on to the belief that we would be well.

The hotels around us were very quiet. Large conferences that normally attracted thousands of people were being cancelled, even though many had travelled from the other side of the world. A few days before Disneyland closed its doors to the public, we enjoyed a day on all the rides.

We remained aware of what was happening around us; we watched the news religiously and took precautionary measures to take care of ourselves. We knew we had a long-day stay at the Los Angeles International Airport before commencing a twelve-hour journey back to New Zealand. We invested in the airport lounge to stay away from the massive crowds, and then we journeyed home.

The entire time we stood with faith instead of fear. We believed we would be well; we did everything we normally do to take care of our own physical health and ensure our own immune system was strong. We never for a moment felt fear and dread.

We landed safely in New Zealand, walked through the terminal alongside thousands and thousands of arriving passengers. By this stage, it was the middle of March 2020, and cases of Covid-19 had been coming into the country for many days, including the day we landed and the days to follow.

I watched the newspapers for several weeks to observe where all the Covid cases were coming from, and on which flights they arrived. Finally, I stopped looking, but I did observe that there were no cases arriving on our flight. Yes, there were Covid cases on flights from Los Angeles just before ours and afterward on the same day, but not on our flight.

The one thing I decided to do was not to fall into a place of fear with the virus. Did it mean I didn't take it seriously? Of course not. Grant and I both took it very seriously. It did mean, however, that we chose not to focus on fear but believe that we would be taken care of.

This is how I have navigated through the entire pandemic, choosing not to be fearful. I have taken responsibility for my own physical wellness, immune system, sanitising, and physical distancing, without dumping that responsibility on anyone else. It has meant that instead of focusing on daily television broadcasts or excessive media about the state of the world, I chose to focus on something else to feed my mind.

Did it mean that I didn't pay attention to what was going on? No, it meant I focused on faith and not on fear when it came to the state of the world. It meant I believed that all would be as it was meant to be, that all would be well in my world if I just let go and went with the flow of life.

It meant that I was able to enjoy the day, the present moment, and see the joy around me instead of focusing on a pandemic and what the state of the world might be like next year or in five years. I continued to practise everything I had already written about. This moment, I focus on my life and what I can control without obsessing about what is happening around me.

When I reflect on the life my parents endured during World War II—the hunger, the fear of bombers flying over their homes, the sound of my father's mother being taken away and murdered, the feeling of my mother's frozen feet because she had no shoes, the fact she shared a bed with all her siblings, my father losing his brother in the war, and more—I am so grateful for mine.

What we experience is frustrating, but one day at a time, everything is manageable. With my faith in God, I can live in a state of peace and gratitude, even during a global pandemic.

Like many others in the world, I am still unspeakably grateful to have a roof over my head, food to eat, warmth, family, but above all, my faith in a person greater than myself. God is mightier than any pandemic.

Chapter: 60

Discovering Your Own Winning Formula

There is a favourite quote I found several decades ago by St. Francis de Sales. He said, "Do not lose your inner peace for anything whatsoever, not even if your whole world seems upset. If you find that you have wandered away from the shelter of God, lead your heart back to Him quietly and simply."

No matter what is happening in my life, I must remain calm and unmoved by the uncertainty it brings. If I lose my calmness or peace of mind, even for a moment, I must do everything I can to regain it. I know, intellectually and from experience, that I cannot solve anything, or even think straight, when I am agitated.

Anger, resentment, and anxiety, plus all those other negative emotions that can steal your peace, are emotional homes I do my best not to dwell in. Does it mean I don't go there? No. My automatic go-to emotion in the past was often anger, undergirded by sadness. I felt everything deeply, and at times I still do.

I now know that slipping into a negative place and remaining there is a pattern I must not allow myself to indulge in anymore.

Taking the time to quieten my mind, to find that stillness and peace and communion with God, for whatever time it takes, must come first. I will accomplish more by doing this than by being in a hurried state full of activities of a long day.

First, I know not to do anything that will take me away from the uncertainty and discomfort of the present moment. This means I do not run away to food, business, or projecting my feelings onto something or someone else.

Instead, it may mean going for a gentle walk. I might write in my journal, or it might mean opening my gratitude journal and adding to it or reading entries from previous days. It may mean opening some of my favourite spiritual books and sayings, or even listening to them, to help me change my state of mind. It may be something as simple as saying, *Thank you, God, for removing from me this feeling that I have no control over right now. Thank you for helping me to feel your peace and joy within my heart right now. Thank you, God, for remembering me right now.*

Life happens to us all, and it will continue to happen. What I have written in this book are the tools and strategies that I use to live this one precious, magnificent life. It isn't always easy, but each day I know to do something. Over time, I have discovered the winning formula that works for me.

Why do I do it? The alternative is not as nice, and I have a strong reason why it is important for me to cherish life. Not everyone has the privilege to live a long life. So far, I have, and I choose to embrace it. I invite you to also craft your own winning formula. If you are currently searching, feeling that the time has come to discover what faith means to you, then take the time now. Learn what surrender means, what letting go means. Discover your own path to acceptance and calm.

This topic is not something I have ever wanted to push on someone else. I made my own decisions and let others observe or follow if they chose. If asked how to find faith, then I share what works for me.

If you feel confused on your search, take time to be still, and during your stillness, pray, meditate, and open yourself up to the flow of life. Soon, life will bring you what you need to see, hear, or feel.

Many come to a place of searching when they have hit a wall, when they have experienced incredible loss in their lives, when they have hit rock bottom. This is when they say, *I can't, He can, so I am going to let Him.* Some then go on to say, *whoever He is.*

When we stop racing around trying to control and fix things and have the courage to look within, this is when we finally find our formula for peace and getting ourselves together. As the story goes, when we get ourselves together, then our whole world comes together. The thing is, if we keep running from life and do not go within, then we risk going without.

If this is the journey you are on, take one step at a time and do your best to let go and allow the flow of life. Follow your intuition, listening and feeling what is right for you.

Ultimately, your spiritual life will be a place not where you are forced to go, or must go when you are suffering. Nor should it be a path to follow because you feel obligated to take it because others are, or others say you must. It is a beautiful place you want to go. A place of surrender, peace, and calm, where you are you, and no one else.

Conclusion

Walking beside another human being as they face the end stage of their lives is not for the faint-hearted. Yet, nothing has surpassed the work I have done with those beautiful people who have now passed away. To say that it has been an honour is an understatement.

Since the completion of this book, my father Smiljan, aka Smiley, passed away, as did my precious mother, Pavica, eight months later. I have feared the passing of my parents all my life, since I was a little girl. It is as if the past two decades have prepared me to be able to sit with my parents as they return home to God.

Where there was once fear, I have now turned to a place of acceptance. Acceptance of life on life's terms, which includes death. Death is the price we pay for life, just as grief is the price we pay for love.

I didn't always feel this way; it has been a long, beautiful, and challenging path to come to this place where I am now—to be so present during this heartbreaking time. Knowing that death will come is the one gift I hold to help me live this one precious life and to also encourage others to as well. We think we are indestructible until we are given the life lesson that we are not.

No matter what we have been through in our lives, no matter how many times we feel life has knocked us down, it is how many times we get back up again that matters. We all have greatness within us, and we all deserve to live fully, passionately, and joyfully.

What I have discovered is that the greatest way to serve God and mankind is to keep getting up and never give up.

I invite you to do the same.

Citations

Frankl, Viktor E. (1984), *Man's Search for Meaning.* New York: Washington Square Press.

Kubler-Ross, Elisabeth. (1989), *On Death and Dying.* London and New York: Tavistock / Routledge

Life Application Bible. (1988), *The Living Bible.* Wheaton, Illinois: Tyndale House Publishers, Inc. and Youth for Christ, USA.

Made in the USA
Columbia, SC
01 July 2025

2207cacc-6c7e-4e88-aa85-4c80bc96467fR01

INCORPORATING

IN

VIRGINIA

•WITHOUT A LAWYER•

Published by Consumer Publishing Incorporated

9317 Barrington Blvd. SW
Knoxville, TN 37922-6210
615-690-0416

First Printing. Revised Edition. July 1991

INTRODUCTION - PLEASE READ

We want to express our appreciation to the State Corporation Commission for their time. Producing this book without their help would have been difficult.

We have done everything possible to insure the accuracy of this kit, but please be aware that laws and procedures are constantly changing, and subject to different interpretations. So, for protection in a litigious society, Consumer Publishing, Inc., nor anyone associated with this book makes any guarantee or warranty about the information it contains, or information obtained through the telephone help line. Also, the Corporation Commission of Virginia is not responsible for the contents of this book. The responsibility of starting and running a corporation rests with you. Use of this book and related information will constitute agreement with these terms.

This book was constructed so the pages could be removed easily. It is constructed similar to a "scratch" pad. The forms are as easily removed from this kit as a sheet is torn from a scratch pad. All you need to do is open the book to the page you wish to remove. Then, while holding that page, open the kit as far as possible until the front and back covers are touching each other, and gently pull your form out. If you choose to, you may photocopy the forms instead of removing them. If you have difficulty removing any pages, or damage any while removing them, please call us and replacements will be sent immediately. Also, you'll need to make copies of forms before writing on them so you'll have extras if you make a mistake. You will definitely need to make copies of the minutes and consents in section five, as you will use these pages in keeping records for the corporation and will need extras as time goes by.

We feel it necessary to make a note about the gender references used in this manual. We realize that a great number of women start and succeed in their own business, but for simplicities sake, the references in this book are to "he" and "him". We hope you understand.

If you have any questions about this manual, need clarification, or have a comment, feel free to call. We'll be glad to assist, but are unable to provide legal advice. Our telephone number is (615) 690-0416. The help line hours are from 3 - 5 Pm, M - F E.S.T.

Thank you for purchasing this book.